CHAOS CLEAR
AS GLASS

CHAOS CLEAR AS GLASS

A MEMOIR

ANN HYMAN

FOREWORD BY EUGENIA PRICE

LONGSTREET PRESS
Atlanta, Georgia

Published by
LONGSTREET PRESS, INC.
2150 Newmarket Parkway
Suite 102
Marietta, Georgia 30067

Printed in the United States of America

1st printing 1991

Library of Congress Catalog Card Number 90-063899

ISBN 0-929264-89-4

This book was printed by R. R. Donnelley & Sons, Harrisonburg,
Virginia. The text was set in Modern Roman by Coghill Book
Typesetting, Richmond, Virginia. Cover Design by Laura Ellis.
Cover illustration by Trevor Stone Irvin.
Text design by Jill Dible.

For Henry Hyman, and for his children

FOREWORD

My friend Ann Hyman is a writer gifted with the rare ability to turn a chaotic event, a tragic or merely puzzling or ordinary event, from something we don't know how to fit into the pattern of our lives into a felt experience "as clear as glass." This certainly isn't news to anyone along the south-eastern coast who looks first, as do I, for Ann Hyman's column or feature in the widely read *Florida Times-Union.* Like mine, Ann's readers are stubbornly loyal. And well we may be, because Ann has the knack of leading us directly to the heart of things. I find myself reading her column not because I'm always interested in its often local subject, but because I know Ann wrote it. The piece may concern a rock concert held in Jacksonville, Florida (which interests me not at all), but I read because from it, I know I'll glean some nugget which throws light on the scope of Ann herself and that *always* interests me.

Without doubt, the woman has a way of making "chaos clear as glass." Many can write, few in my opinion, with a style that invariably illumines. Clarifies. Stands upright. Gives new insight. Amuses. Indeed, as I went eagerly through manuscript pages of *Chaos Clear as Glass,* I marveled that plain or chaotic or happy or sad times in my long life seemed to clear up for me because of what Ann wrote in these pages from her own life.

Some writers are lucid, others entertain, still others cause us to think, to weigh our own actions and reactions, give spiritual insights. Seldom does one writer have the skills to make all those things happen.

From my heart, I promise—not only to you who read my books but to anyone who treats himself or herself to *Chaos Clear as Glass*—that new and many-faceted thoughts will come to you as you read. Ann takes us to strange and different locales, but she also journeys to places so dear and so familiar to us all that it is very like going home again. You will find yourself here, you will also find family members and friends who can still stir your heart. People who can drive us up the wall are here too. *Chaos Clear as Glass* can be read if you want only to escape, to be entertained. It can also be read and reread if you want to learn, to think. It can be read again (I've been through it three times, reveling in the rewards!) if you're lonely or sad or troubled or just plain exhilarated by this phenomenon we call living. Whatever your need, Ann Hyman will probably meet it, as she's met so many of my needs through the years in which we've known and loved each other. She vows I urged her to write this book. If I did, good for me! It was she who planted the seed for my own novel, *Margaret's Story,* and I was pleased as punch that she mentioned it in these pages. By now, you must believe that I consider Ann Hyman one of our truly important writers and, as a human being, one of God's great ladies.

I asked, in fact, to write the foreword to *Chaos Clear as Glass* because I'm eager for you to know her too. Selecting gift books is seldom easy these days because sensibilities can be easily scarred by writing that shocks or depresses or leaves us feeling as though the very least we can do for the poor, morbid-minded author is to offer to commit suicide. I can honestly tell you that I can think of no type of person all the way from those who fancy themselves among the reading elite to those who long for clean simplicity and good, healthy escape who will not like Ann's efforts. Efforts? You bet writing is an effort, but you'd never know it is for Ann because her style is not only uniquely hers, it sings and chuckles and stirs and always, in some small or large way, leaves richer.

This has been pure pleasure for me being allowed to present to you, to your mind and heart, *Chaos Clear as Glass,* by my valued, perceptive friend and fellow scribe, Ann Hyman.

—Eugenia Price
St. Simons Island, Georgia

PREFACE

In 1974, anthropologists working in Ethiopia discovered a three-million-year-old sift of bones that turned out to be the oldest and most complete skeleton of our distant cousin, *Australopithecus afarensis,* ever unearthed. They called her Lucy, after the heroine of the Beatles' song "Lucy in the Sky with Diamonds," and they also called her, in Ethiopian, Dinquinesh, which means "thou art wonderful."

Someone said, and I think it may have been Flannery O'Connor, though I'm not sure she said it first, that a writer's true work is to name the things of God.

I don't think the task is exclusively the work of writers, nor that the things named need be only the sorts of things that we commonly understand as the things of God. It's simpler. It is the work of all of us to name things, all the things, jackknives, antelopes, transistors, Lucy. That is how we begin to make order of chaos.

It's easier to do in the world than in our heads.

We can all agree what to call an object or phenomenon, and that's that. But the stuff our lives are made of is more elusive. Half the time we don't know what to call it. It's got no name, and we don't know where it fits the pattern or even if there is a pattern.

But there are those few, fine moments when it all comes clear, when you could swear that life is not chaos after all, but journey, a journey with purpose, and one that may even come out right. There are those moments when you swear you can see through the chaos as if it were glass. This book is about some of those moments and how they happened.

Chaos Clear as Glass would not have happened at all without my friend Eugenia Price. She suggested it in the first place and kept on believing that I could write this book, that it was worth the writing, when I would have tossed half a manuscript on the shelf and never gotten back to it. I simply cannot measure nor adequately acknowledge how I have treasured her praise and encouragement and generous gifts of time during the writing of this book. But I can say thanks, and I do.

I wish also to thank my colleagues at the *Florida Times-Union,* especially Features Editor Sarah Wood. I have had many, many opportunities through the newspaper to explore the world in ways I would not otherwise have seen it, and I have been trusted to write about it as I have seen it.

Ghosting

1

Ghosting has nothing to do with chasing the spirits of the dead. Ghosting is the process of looking for ourselves in all the places where we used to be. It's about the way we were and how we got to be the way we are.

When I moved to Jacksonville, Florida, in 1959, I lived in a little furnished apartment on an unpretentious, respectable street, at a down-at-the-heels corner of the Riverside neighborhood. There were three apartments in the building. A real family—mom, dad, kids—lived downstairs. I shared an upstairs apartment with a college chum. Our other neighbor was an intriguing bachelor—tall and dark, an older man (forty!), who wore a trench coat and told tales of his years in Europe and India and who had a copy of *America as a Civilization* on his coffee table.

I cruised through the old neighborhood recently. I stopped at the old address. I inventoried, in my mind, the upstairs apartments, circa 1959. Bleached blond furniture and driftwood lamps. Kidney-shaped ashtrays on wrought-iron legs, for crying out loud. Dave Brubeck and Johnny Mathis on the hi-fi.

I almost climbed the narrow stairs, knocked on the door and said to whoever opened: "Hey, I used to live here." But, I couldn't figure out what I'd say next, and I didn't feel all that comfortable about who might answer the door, so I kept going.

I drove past the dark, hole-in-the-wall grocery store where we used to buy cigarettes and Orbit beer. An old man sat on an upturned box outside the front door, soaking in some morning sun, sipping coffee.

The neighborhood is shabbier, tougher; the streets are looking mean.

But when you're ghosting, you're not looking at the present, at how things have changed. You're looking for the past, at things that have remained the same.

Down the street from the grocery is a doughnut shop that is a fifties classic. Heck, classic nothing. It's a masterpiece, down to the tin awnings and the neon and the tile floor.

The kid who runs the place now says that people come in all the time and try to put the place back together the way they remember it. In their minds they shove the coolers and counter back where they remember it.

A customer grins, nods, says he used to go without milk at lunchtime at West Riverside Elementary so he could buy a doughnut on his way home. On his birthday he didn't want cake. He wanted doughnuts.

The kid behind the counter pours another splash of coffee into the man's cup.

You probably weren't even born then, the man tells the kid.

The kid shrugs.

For sure he wasn't born when the mysterious stranger and I were drinking coffee at the counter and smoking Pall Malls and talking, talking, talking, sliding into the future.

I bought a doughnut for old times' sake.

I'm going ghosting. You come too.

There is a landscape of the past in our minds that we can explore, fine-tune, interpret and reinterpret. It is a landscape of images, people, voices, places to reclaim from memory, to spin and weave into the pattern of the present.

It has its claim on us.

It is a special grace if the claim is peaceful.

Hopewell is a little community of orange groves and strawberry fields in Hillsborough County, several miles south of Plant City, near where Florida 60 and Florida 39 cross. It was settled in 1870 by John and Sally McDonald. They had five childen—Walter, Sally, Glenn, Molly, and Lucy Anna. Lucy Anna, the baby of the family, was called "Pet" by her parents and her brothers and sisters.

Her bridegroom, Simpson Edmondson, came down with yellow fever on their wedding day and was so close to death that, they said later, the Angel of Death was already in the room when Simpson rose up in his sickbed and declared, "I'm not a-gonna die. I'm a-gonna live and I'm a-gonna marry Miss Pet."

That's exactly how it happened. He married Miss Pet in 1888. She was my grandmother. When I was a child, I used to go with my grandmother every summer, and sometimes at Christmas and in the spring, to visit Hopewell.

This is the homeplace, she told me.

Homeplace. Sweet, sweet word that falls on the ear almost as if from another language, an old language that we do not speak anymore but still understand.

In the summertime, after supper, we would sit out on Aunt Molly's front porch—waiting for a breath of air, as the old folks put it—and they would talk to one another and I would listen. Their words washed around me, a gentle current bearing names of people who were dead before I was born, tales of the Civil War, of times in Alabama before they came to Hopewell, of the Florida frontier, of summer nights when John McDonald led his flock to prayer meeting, walking at the head of the procession, holding a lantern to light their way down the dirt road to the little Baptist church they helped build almost as soon as they planted their grove and called the place Hopewell. It was called after a place in Virginia, where they had lived before Alabama and they had called the place in Virginia after a place in England where someone had begun. Or so they told the story.

Oral history. It comes down to long evenings on a dark porch, listening to the old folks talk, nestled among them like a sleepy pup, absorbing memories of where we have come from and who we are. It is the growing sense of belonging among them, as if we have come from those times and places, too. It is words, words, words soaking down into our consciousness and deeper, like rain making its way through the limestone to an underground river.

The river flows on and on, hidden, leading always out of the past into the present. Continuity.

After almost forty years, I decide that I want to see Hopewell again. What do I expect to find? Condos, I suppose. Mobile home villages. Convenience stores. Distant cousins who are strangers. Forty years is a long time, after all, and nothing stays the same, especially not little Florida hamlets that are all but in the shadow of Tampa's skyscrapers now.

The Hopewell Baptist Church is not the same. The old church is still somewhere at the heart of the building, but the plain, sweet country meeting house has been swallowed up in improvements. There have been additions—colonial columns, stained glass windows, a wide porch, a vestibule, a steeple. It's set back in a grove of oaks, pretty as a picture. It's just not the picture I carry in my mind—of a little white clapboard church with plain glass windows and two entrances because long, long ago men and women entered the church, and sat, separately. That's old-time country Baptist. "Men on one side and women on the other," says Isabel Preacher. "I declare. Well, we kind of got over that."

Isabel Preacher is a lifelong member of the church. She unlocks the door and shows me around. She points to a portrait hanging in the vestibule over an old pulpit that has been refinished and polished to a dark, rich glow.

"Walter McDonald," she says. "And that was his pulpit."

Walter McDonald was pastor of the church for forty-five years, from 1888 until 1933. He was my grandmother's brother. He died before I was born, but his was one of the names that drifted on the current of words that flowed across Aunt Molly's porch.

I study the old photograph. Black eyes, a nose like a hawk. Wire-rimmed spectacles. A shock of gray hair and a drooping handlebar mustache. A good face. Strong. Lively. A sociable kind of face.

"He had spirit and power," Mrs. Preacher says. "What rings in my ears, I can hear him just clap his hands together and shout out, 'By grace 'ere you saved, through faith and not of yourself!' Oh, he was just real dear and precious to us. He demanded deep respect. You just didn't go against him."

Isabel Preacher grew up in the church while Uncle Walter was preaching. He baptized her in a little creek about a quarter-mile south of the church, and a few months before he died in 1933 he officiated at her wedding.

Continuity.

A narrow road winds past the church, orange groves on one side, open fields on the other. 'Most everybody who lives along the road has connections to the McDonald family, or the Bugg family, who moved to Hopewell in 1878.

Thelma Bugg, who lives just down the road from the church, is both. Like me, she is John McDonald's great-granddaughter, and her husband was a member of the Bugg clan. She has sent word to Mrs. Preacher that she wants to meet me.

We have never met before, at least not that either of us remembers. But, oh, I've seen her before, or at least her image. She steps out on the front porch when she hears the car pull up. Blood. DNA. The double helix—a continuum. It could be my grandmother standing there. The black eyes, the white hair, the skin, the smile, the way she stands with her arms folded, holding to her elbows. The voice.

"Lucy!" she says, referring to my mother. "Why, it could be Lucy standing there. And I used to love it so when Lucy came to visit. She was so much fun."

"And you," I say. "You look just like my grandmother—"

"Aunt Pet," she murmurs.

She takes me into the house and we sit in the parlor for a while and finally end up in the kitchen and I ask her if she knows the family chicken-and-dumplings recipe. Every-body's grandmother, I suppose, made something that was food for the soul, the stuff of legend, a recollection that lingers long after the cook is dust—culinary immortality. In Miss Pet's case, the legacy is the memory of her chicken and dumplings.

It occurs to me, in Thelma's kitchen, that just maybe my grandmother learned from her mother. Maybe Thelma, closer to the heart of things in Hopewell, got in on the secret.

She nods. Use chicken fat instead of shortening for the dumplings, she says.

I write it down, eagerly. But I never use the recipe.

Recipes, formulas are for conjuring tricks, not sacraments. It is intent that validates a sacrament, or, in the case of the chicken and dumplings, it's memory.

The road in front of Thelma's house winds around to the homeplace, where John and Sally McDonald and their offspring lived for four generations, where Aunt Molly lived when I was growing up and used to come to visit.

It is a pretty old Florida farmhouse, a little in need of fixing up. The side porch and the front porch are busy with Victorian gingerbread. A gallery runs around the back of the house to the kitchen, serving as a sort of open hall past bedrooms, parlor, dining room.

Dorothy and Roy Hull live next to the old house, on the same property. Roy is Aunt Molly's grandson. We know one another and talk comfortably about the present and about the past.

Mainly the past.

"I hadn't thought about those old days in a long time. It feels good, remembering," Roy says.

We talk about Aunt Molly's country kitchen, big enough for three stoves—wood, electric, and oil. She used all of them, cooking different things on different stoves. She said that an electric stove was fine for frying bacon, but a wood stove was needed to bake.

Roy remembers that she kept a flour sack of cookies in the pie safe to pass out to the children when they came home from school.

We remember the pump on the back porch, outside the kitchen.

"You could pump water in a glass, and it would sweat the glass," Roy says.

"That was the best water to drink!" Thelma nods. "It was real good-tasting."

So it had been special after all. Nostalgia, sentimentality hadn't played any tricks on me. I did not remember that the water was so cold coming out of the ground that it would bead a glass. In fact, I did not remember ever drinking it from a glass. I remembered a dipper, sharing a common dipper and pumping the water into an oaken bucket and how you did not return what you did not drink from the dipper to the bucket. It was proper etiquette to throw what was left out the back door, to send a quicksilver wing of water arching into the clean-swept dooryard, where it beaded in the dust.

I had not remembered the glass sweating, but now I remember the cold lip of the dipper against my mouth, the slight metallic taste of the water and the oak taste from the bucket, water complex as fine wine.

A year after my visit to Hopewell I remember Aunt Molly's dipper again. I'm in the Soviet Union, and I see, for the first time, the drinking water dispensers that are equipped with a single glass. You drop in two kopeks and mineral water is dispensed into the glass. After you drink, you give the glass a couple of plunges past some brushes set in a little sudsy water and put it back under the spout for the next customer. Not many Westerners are likely to get that thirsty.

But we all used to drink out of the same well, so to speak, to share a common dipper. I think of the waterboys running out onto the field at high-school football games, carrying a sloshing bucket of water and the grimy boys under the tall lights of the stadium pouring the water over their heads to cool down and gulping from the dipper and spitting the water onto the ground and passing the dipper to a teammate.

Dippers, the sharing of the common cup. I wonder whether the water dispensers on the streets in Moscow mean that the Russians share a greater sense of community, of brotherhood, of common origin and destiny than we do. Or whether it is simply a matter of greater fastidiousness, of higher public health awareness in the West, or whether we simply have more money and paper to spend on individual cups and cans and bottles and so on. I think the answer is yes. Yes, yes, and yes.

Our conversation moves from water to wine.

Aunt Molly kept a cupboard of homemade blackberry wine for medicinal purposes. And that's no euphemism. The old ladies were dyed-in-the-wool, if not foot-washin', Baptists, and they were serious about their teetotaling.

That's not to say they were without their vices.

"Grandma and Aunt Pet both dipped snuff, you know," Roy says. "'Course, they were ashamed to go buy it for themselves, so they'd pay a boy a nickel to buy it for them, and they'd have their snuff."

Bless them both.

The last time the sisters saw one another my grandmother was in her eighties and Aunt Molly was ninety. As my grandmother came up the steps to the front porch of the homeplace, Aunt Molly opened the door.

"You've brought me my baby sister," she said. "You've brought me my Pet."

They've been dead and in their graves for decades, turned to bones and lace, a cameo, a gold band, a wisp of white hair like a halo around a skull. Yet we have called them forth by our talk of cold well water and snuff and blackberry wine.

"You've brought me my baby sister. You've brought me my Pet."

It is just sunset when Dorothy and Roy and I walk out into the yard.

"Would you like to see the old house?" Dorothy asks.

The entry hall has been closed off at one end so that it does not go straight through to the back gallery anymore. The front bedroom where my grandmother and I slept has been turned into a sitting room.

Well, what had I expected?

Everything changes.

And then I step across the hall into Aunt Molly's room and back through forty years.

The same pictures hang on the walls. The plain iron bedstead and the oak dresser are the same. The sewing rockers are in place in front of the little fireplace, one on each side of the hearth, where the sisters sat and talked at the end of the day and had their snuff.

I cannot breathe. I am still, so still, to feel, to hear, almost to see through the veil between . . . between the present and the timeless, the tapestry that holds first the pattern and then the image.

It feels as if Molly and Miss Pet are just out of sight, as if they stepped down the gallery to the kitchen a moment ago.

I feel that if I am very quiet, and listen, I might hear the distant voice of a child playing in the yard, just at the edge of the darkening grove, and it will be my own voice, answering the call to come home for supper.

2

All of us would like to change the past, to rewrite what the moving finger has already written long ago, so long that the ink is faded, the words illegible, raw images turned to unintelligible metaphor.

We have many labels for changing the past, an entire pop industry devoted to it. Depending on our frame of reference, we label it psychoanalysis or the healing of memories or tending the inner child. We have encounter groups and support groups and recovery groups and quest seminars promising enlightenment payoffs that range from coal-walking to confrontation with God and karma.

I guess it's all good for the soul, like confession.

I got in on the end of an Oprah show one afternoon.

"So, what's it today?" I ask my daughter.

"People who have sex with animals," she says.

"No kidding—" I study the ordinary-looking faces on the tube more carefully. "Still?"

"Recovering," Lizzie says.

Recovering. I love it.

Where do they find these people? Does a producer run an ad in the classifieds? Sex with animals? Call 1-800-DIS-GUST.

Doing it in the first place is less surprising than getting on television and telling it. I dunno. What a world, what a world.

Putting ourselves together.

Changing the past.

We can't, of course, actually change the past. What we're really after is to fix it, going back to the bit of the tapestry that has come undone or is badly stitched and catching up the loose threads, reweaving the burned spot, bleaching out the stain.

Restoration.

Reconstruction.

Filling in some missing places.

I live in a neighborhood that is on the National Register of Historic Places, and there's a homeowners' association that fights rezoning and parking lots and high rises and four-laning roads and cutting down trees, and it does whatever it takes to keep us kind of quaint. The old places, indeed, have their charm, but they need a lot of looking after.

Changing the past, I think, is also a matter of restoration, of preservation, of finally going back and looking after un-finished business, of filling in some cracks and chunks that got gouged out along the way.

It's the polishing up, the rewrite.

It's the time in our life when we begin to understand the characters, to make sense of the plot, and maybe notice the foreshadowing.

I have a little bundle of letters that my grandfather sent to my grandmother. Most were written near the beginning of the century, and they have the intriguing look that everyday things acquire if they are saved past their own time. They are faded and look mysterious and romantic.

They are neither.

My grandfather liked to take the baths in Hot Springs, Arkansas, every so often and to spend part of the summer in the North Georgia hills. He was dutiful about writing home, and he reported prosaically on the cost of travel, the quality of food at his lodgings, the state of his health. He asked about the children and the orange grove and the kinfolk and handed out advice wherever it seemed needed. There is nothing dramatic to be learned of family history from the letters.

There are, however, a few subtle things to be learned about the people. The letters illuminate, though slightly, a man and a woman as individuals and as husband and wife in ways that their children and grandchildren never saw.

I did not know my grandfather. He died the year I was born. But I spent every hour I could in my grandmother's shadow, a biddy bonded to the mother hen, watching, listening, following her into a world that she shaped the way she wanted it shaped, according to an old pattern that pleased her. Oh yes. She moved to town when her house at the grove burned, but she kept her country ways. She churned her own butter, put up pickles and jelly and figs and spiced peaches. She *preserved*—times, ways of doing, tales.

When she was a little girl, her mother told her about the way the Yankee soldiers came to the farm in Alabama and ran off the stock and rode their horses up and down the rows of corn to ruin it and pulled all the bedding out of the house and tore it up with their bayonets and stole the chickens.

But they didn't burn the house.

When she told the story, Sally McDonald always added the tag line. It was her debt of gratitude to a Yankee trooper who didn't do his worst one day in Alabama.

So, Mr. Shakespeare, what do you say to that? The good that men do is not necessarily interred with the bones after all—and little stories can last a long, long time.

Maybe the mirror image of the story exists in somebody's store of family lore in Ohio, a recollection of a farm woman in Alabama who touched a man's heart or his conscience because she reminded him of his own women, back home, trying to run a dairy or an apple orchard alone while he soldiered through the South.

That is the moment in her life when Sally McDonald lives in my mind, that moment when the Yankees came and didn't burn her house. I must say they're the only Yankees I've ever heard of who didn't burn the house.

They burned the big house at Middleburg plantation near Charleston, South Carolina. There's a gentling heap of rubble still scattered around the massive stump of a ruined chimney, a mound of shards and prickly vines.

"You'd think, in a hundred years, they'd have cleaned this up," my husband said, pushing a toe through the pink dust.

I shook my head. "Never."

That heap of rubble might look like a heap of rubble to most folks, but to some of us it looks like we've come a long, long way together.

Tell me a story.

Tell me who I am.

Where did I come from?

My grandmother's stories stretched back and back and further back. But I never saw her as a girl or as a young woman. In my mind, somehow, she was always already old—white-haired, widowed, something of a recluse.

I guess what strikes me about these ordinary letters is that they offer a glimpse of Miss Pet as other than an old woman. They reflect her concern for her young daughters and for her aging parents and her plans to visit them—in Hopewell—during my grandfather's stay in Arkansas. In her letters I see how many chapters of her life passed long before I was born. I see that she was many, many people before she was my grandmother.

I note, in the early letters, my grandfather greeted her, "My dearest Pet," and closed, "Your loving Simpson." The last letter in the bundle comes twenty years after the first. "Dearest Mama," he wrote, and he closed, "Love, Papa."

She was seventeen when they married. He was twenty-three. She told me once that, had he died in a year she would never have married again. She loved him that much. Or so she said.

Well—

He died when he was seventy-one. The Angel of Death stood in the room that day, she told me. "He raised up in the bed, and he said to me, 'Don't you see him there—there at the foot of the bed?' But nobody else would see the Angel of Death, only Papa—"

"This bed, Mama?" I asked her, gazing at the space where her hands rested on the dark polished curve of the foot-board, the place where the angel must have stood and rested incandescent fingers, waiting to touch Papa and to take his soul to heaven.

"This bed." She nodded.

Odd, huh?

The Angel of Death had been there before, on their wedding day, forty-one years before. "But I'm not a-gonna die," Simpson Edmondson said. "I'm not a-gonna die. I'm a-gonna live and I'm a-gonna marry Miss Pet."

3

Unless it's been torn down to make way for a condo in the last year, there's a big old derelict beach house sagging on its pilings on Anna Maria Island, on Florida's gulf coast. The seawall is gone, and when the tide is very high, the gulf laps around its feet. The snaggle-tooth stairs hanging off the porch are rotten, don't even reach the ground anymore. Windows are busted out. A curtain flaps out of one of them like a signal of surrender.

Every now and then an enterprising feature writer spots a story in the old place and reports that the house is haunted. He finds somebody who claims to see lights moving around the house at midnight, to hear strange sounds when the moon is full and the wind is wild, that sort of thing.

When I was a kid, our family used to spend summers in that big old house. So I figure maybe we're the ghosts, me and my brother and sister, an aunt and uncle, a couple of cousins, my mother and father, the yellow and white dog, Trixie. Some of us aren't dead yet, but I figure it's our impressions, not our spirits, hanging around the place, doing summer reruns.

I think of us as actors in an old movie, faded images that will finally disappear in a cloud of dust when the bulldozers push down the old summer place to make way for a condo.

Poof.

We'll be gone like a puff of dandelion.

In my earliest recollections of the island, I recall only a few houses scattered along the beach. Big, weathered, shingled houses built up on pilings, with screen porches that were wide and deep and jumbled with wicker rockers and canvas chairs and maybe a three-seater wooden swing hung from the rafters on creaking chains. A stand of Australian pine was planted around most of the houses, the loose white sand beneath the pines carpeted with soft brown needles and tiny cones the size and shape of the balls on a curtain fringe. Hammered between two of our pines was a length of sway-backed, gray-weathered wood. On it we cleaned the fish brought in from the gulf and pried open scallops, freeing one perfect bite from each. And then we scrubbed the altar clean.

At the beach we had an icebox. An *icebox.* Imagine! Every few days an ice truck appeared at the door, and an iceman threw back the stiff, patched shroud of heavy canvas that protected his wares from the summer sun. He dug his tongs into a great, smoking block of ice and hoisted it into the kitchen.

My mother worried whether that icebox was really keeping anything cold enough and grumbled that the drip pan beneath it always needed to be emptied. A kaleidoscope pattern of fissures bloomed deep in the ice when it was first broken. Fat mullet wrapped in soggy newspaper sunk into the melting ice block. The ice pick was driven into a splintery place on the kitchen wall, always handy.

It was another time.

The summers all run into one another. The first batch— the icebox batch—was also the batch of the blackouts. There were heavy dark shades at every window against enemy submarines. Coast Guardsmen with rifles and a dog patrolled the beach at night. We believed the dog had been trained to kill but would not kill Americans.

The Coast Guardsmen came to our door once because my mother had hung a girdle in the window to dry, and in the moonlight it was visible from the beach. Like a signal, they worried. That sounds funny now. Actually, it sounded funny then, but it was also very serious business. It was World War II. Real serious business. Once a yellow rubber life raft floated up in front of our house. It was empty, and we told one another that the airman had been rescued, was safe somewhere. We wanted to keep the raft, but the Coast Guardsmen came and took it away.

Time passed. The Coast Guardsmen and the blackout curtains were gone. More houses, two inns, a few apartments were built on the island, and the rickety old wooden bridge was pulled down to make way for a wide, smooth new bridge.

We changed, too.

We gave up reading war comics and keeping a lookout for enemy submarines and took up movie magazines. Esther Williams and Peter Lawford made a movie on our island. We cheated at Monopoly and had a season of seances, disturbing Abe Lincoln's rest all summer long. He was the only dead person we knew. We began to get interested in boys, and, somewhat later, boys began to get interested in us. We sneaked a beer every now and then. We sneaked cigarettes every chance we got.

But some things didn't change. Fishing. With cane poles. Floating in patched innertubes above the offshore reef, a tilting bucket of fiddler crabs for bait drifting among us, a croker sack tethered to each tube to hold our catch. We got angel fish, sheepshead, grunts. It's a wonder the sharks didn't get us.

Each summer my father led the harvest of scallops from the bay. He didn't like to fish, but he liked to scallop, so it was his annual marine event. On the appointed day we went down a twisty washboard road on the east side of the island to the edge of the bay. There, like Moses leading the Children of Israel into the Red Sea, my father led us out across the mud flats and into the water to fill our buckets with elusive prey. We wore shoes to protect against stingrays and oyster beds, and our eyes ached from searching past the patterns that danced in the sunstruck water, seeking the scallops hidden in the long, waving grass. They seemed to sense when we reached for them and squirted past our fingers in a New York second.

But we always managed to get enough for the fish fry.

We brought home our buckets and dumped out the scallops on the splintered, silvery planks nailed between the pines and popped the sweet white morsels of flesh into a white enamel dishpan and carried the treasure in to chill on the ice.

A family usually had only one fish fry per summer, but every family had one and everybody was invited to everbody else's fish fry. It added up to a lot of fish fries.

Well, not everything changes.

Sure, sure. Causeways and condominiums and fancy restaurants are the island ambience now. The few old houses that are left are clearly doomed, like old rogue elephants already limping off to the graveyard. If anybody's got an icebox in the condo, it likely cost big bucks in an antique shop and isn't used to keep mullet cold.

But the aquamarine gulf and the fine white sand and the sound of the wind in the Australian pines are the same.

And the fish fries.

A bunch of us who grew up spending summers on the island got together for a reunion not long ago. We had a fish fry. We caught all the fish and the scallops and the crabmeat that we ate that night. We talked about the things we were supposed to talk about—what was caught and where and by what bait and method. That fish fry could have happened any time along the years.

Some good people were missing—my father's not here to lead us off to look for scallops anymore, nor my mother to alarm the Coast Guard with her dainties hung out to dry in the moonlight. But, oh, some good new people have come along, and we had a flock of them at the fish fry, from an infant whose arrival came as a shock to her fortyish parents to a bearded kid on his way to join the army.

What changed was our place in the order of things. We're the grownups now. We don't have to sneak beers anymore.

How we haunt our own landscapes.

* * *

The only grave I visit with any regularity is my grandmother's. I never visit the cemetery where my parents are buried. Only rarely do I visit my husband's grave. They're just not there.

It's different with my grandmother.

I think it is because I was there with her during life—every Sunday afternoon we took flowers to the cemetery, arranged blue vases of pink gladiolus at the foot of the substantial marble marker inscribed *Edmondson.* Large, polished slabs of matching marble marked the graves of Papa and Sister—the oldest daughter, who died of pernicious anemia during the thirties.

It was irresistible to jump back and forth between the slabs that covered Papa and Sister, a child's small, thoughtless dance of life among the dead.

"Don't play on the graves," my grandmother corrected me.

And she went on about her work of tending the memory of her husband and her child.

Don't play on the graves.

The last time I visited the cemetery where my grandmother is buried, I was with a friend, and we talked about returning next time I'm in town and bringing a rake and clippers and getting the plot into better trim.

I leaned against the big marker and thought that might be kind of nice. We could bring a picnic, I suggested. I thought I'd like to sit down there, almost with her, and eat a few bites of . . . of bread and butter, I think, and drink from a thermos of cold water.

When summer's over, my chum agreed.

Lucy Anna Edmondson
1871–1956

Her stone matches the others, the ones to which we brought pink gladioli in blue vases.

It's my name, too—Lucy Ann. Nobody will bring gladiolus to me.

We don't live that way anymore. Or at least I do not, nor do my children, so I cannot imagine that they would take up delivering pots of gladiolus to the cemetery after I'm gone.

The departed are just that—departed. Their memory does

not cling to the earth where they are buried, not unless they have imprinted the place in life. I spent time in the old Fogartyville cemetery with my grandmother while she tended her dead, so I can find a trace of her company there now.

My husband never saw the place where he is buried, does not know that his children and I chose it for the trees that mark it because we thought he would like that, to have trees, shade. When I turn into the gates of the cemetery, I get a fix on those trees and they guide me to the place.

Henry Hyman
1918–1981

There is a star of David, the information that he was a first lieutenant in the army during World War II. The marker is the sort to which all veterans are entitled with the thanks of a grateful nation for having, at some time or another, done their duty. The kids and I agreed on it because we thought it appropriate to note that he was a good soldier in a big war because it's important to the world and to us and it was important to him.

History.

Keep in touch, we say.

So we do. We go around and look at the places where things happened.

Lest we forget?

Hey, we don't forget much. It's human nature to remember, and to twist the global into the personal.

Daisy Bonner was a black woman who cooked for President Franklin Roosevelt at the Little White House in Warm Springs, Georgia. There's a photograph of her in the museum there, and you can peek into her room above the garage.

On the day that FDR died—April 12, 1945—she scratched these words, in pencil, on the paneled wall of the kitchen, just above the stove: "Daisy Bonner cooked the first meal and the last one in this cottage for the President Roosevelt."

You can still read her words there, protected now under a little plastic shield fixed to the wall.

With a little research, more could certainly be found out about Daisy Bonner, about the rest of her life. But it isn't the rest of Daisy Bonner's life that catches us. What catches us are those words, scratched on the wall, forty-five years ago. We can almost see her, there in the kitchen, stunned, noting so poignantly, so personally, a convulsion of history, the end of a life, and the part she played in it. She nourished it. We can almost feel the impulse that moved her to write.

It was an impulse to identify herself with something momentous, something that went to the center of her bones, to make certain it was known that she had been there, and why. In part, perhaps, her impulse was to make her mark on history, to note that she had touched one of history's giants. But that was not the greater part of it. The deeper impulse, I think, was to note that history had touched her.

Daisy Bonner's words written on the kitchen wall catch the imagination because they are so personal. Isn't that how history touches us? Personally and specifically. Ask people old enough to have been there what they were doing when the news came that Roosevelt was dead and most can remember.

Scholars may set up shop at Warm Springs and a thousand places like it, places where something happened that the world remembers, looking for history. But I think most of us go to these places looking for ourselves, for little pieces of our lives that were brought into special perspective by larger events. Overheard conversations confirm it. A country woman moves her fingers tenderly over a naval cape like the one FDR so often wore, the one in which he was buried, as she might touch a garment her own father had worn.

Or we may go to places where history was made because we remember stories we were told and the people who told them. The stories, I fancy, have had less to do with what we call history than they have had to do with families. We remember FDR in Warm Springs, but mostly we remember ourselves, and we note how our own lives are woven into the tapestry that holds first the pattern and then the image. We note how we are connected.

Daisy Bonner cooked the first meal and the last in the

cottage at Warm Springs for President Roosevelt. She wanted us to know that.

Henry Hyman was on his way overseas when he found out that FDR was dead. The news crackled over the camp loudspeakers, and he sat down on a curb at Fort Dix, New Jersey, and cried like a baby.

I was lying under a bed in Bradenton, Florida, staring at the bottom of the bed springs, listening to Jack Armstrong, the All-American Boy. I was nine years old.

An announcer interrupted the program and said, "President Roosevelt died today in Warm Springs, Georgia."

I slid out from under the bed and stared at the radio.

The announcer repeated: "President Roosevelt is dead."

I got to the bottom of the stairs at the moment that my father walked in the door.

"President Roosevelt's dead," I announced.

"President Roosevelt? He can't be."

The high drama of having brought the news to the family may have been fate's final little pat on the fertile soil, the splash of the watering can over a seed of journalism that would sprout in due season.

Could be.

The death of FDR was my first scoop, the first sweet taste of The Big Story.

4

Picture Lucy Ann Edmondson Dye like FDR, with a cigarette holder clenched in her teeth at a forty-five-degree angle and a stubborn set to her jaw and the look of a commander-in-chief in her eyes.

There is an idiomatic phrase of love and respect that has been spoken more times than can be reckoned by sentimental, motherless children: "My sainted mother."

My mother was no saint.

She was a force, an elemental force to be reckoned with.

She did not literally look like FDR, you understand. Perhaps it was the cigarette holder that left the impression. Photographs show a young woman with that sullen, haunted beauty that was fashionable in the twenties—the Zelda Fitzgerald look. Later, she had the well-tended look of the television mothers—a plumper model of June Cleaver, complete with sweater dress and white beads. As an old woman, she was cut from the pattern that made Bette Davis—the fierce and defiant and wounded old woman who would have it her way or no way at all.

She could be difficult, as they say.

Indeed.

It would be convention here to say something like this: But she always meant well. I don't know if she did or not. We'd like to think we do, but do any of us *always* mean well?

Sometimes, don't we just plain want our own way? Damn the torpedoes, full speed ahead?

Lucy almost always got her own way. She did it through force of personality. Will. That woman had the strongest will I have ever seen.

There is a family story that, when she was a small child, she once sat in a corner for two days rather than admit wrongdoing. It was her mother who finally declared the truce.

She was powerful, regal. Her subjects strove to please her and all brought her tribute. No one came into her presence empty-handed. Nor did one bring gardenias or Easter lilies. It was understood that she did not care for gardenias or Easter lilies. She would accept Easter lilies. She would not abide gardenias in the house.

She accepted with special pleasure blueberries and an exotic fruit that we called "lady-finger bananas," though I do not know the botanical name. There was a competition in Manatee County to see who would bring Lucy the first blueberries of the season.

One of the last times I saw her, she was in the hospital. She was very old and very frail and her white hair looked like spun glass against the pillow—her own pillow, of course. Hospital issue would not have done. Anyway, a man of prominence—I believe he was a judge—was standing beside her bed, patiently, meticulously manicuring her fingernails.

She did not give that a second thought. Lucy lay there like Cleopatra on her barge and let the judge do her nails.

I can barely imagine a manicurist doing my nails, much less a judge, nor can I imagine anyone combing the farmers' market for the season's first blueberries to lay at my feet.

She had a hold on people, all right. But hers was not a reign of terror.

Well, not in the general understanding of terror. I recall only one spanking. When I was about six years old, we hired a new cook and I waltzed into the kitchen one morning and tested the waters by calling the woman a nigger.

"Ruby Green, you are a big black nigger," I declared.

Lucy overheard.

She snatched me up, turned me over her knee and wore me out. That was that.

When I was older, a teenager, she was not strict or suspicious. She delivered the little talk about trusting me and asked, then, only that I tap gently at her door when I got in at night so that she would know that I was safe.

She was gracious. My friends were always welcome, and they were of genuine interest to her and to my father.

She made wonderful guava and wild plum jelly and pound cake and mayonnaise.

She did her share of good works. During the Depression, she saw children in the schoolyard eating out of garbage cans, and she began immediately to organize a club that literally fed the hungry children of the county and which, to this day, continues to support worthwhile causes. Later, she took up the cause of the arts and ran the props committee of the community theater—probably by intimidation. Heck, no probably about it. She also got the alligators removed from the creek behind the elementary school after half a dog disappeared and people murmured that it could have been a child.

She was loyal to her friends and beloved by them. She was there with the potato salad when there was a funeral, and she came through with a luncheon when there was a wedding.

She liked to have a good time. When she had a couple of drinks, she loved to belt out "Pistol-packin' Mama," and her delivery would have upstaged Ethel Merman.

She was always right.

I remember once that we were sitting in her bedroom when we both spied something flash along the baseboard into her closet. We described it to my father as being as large as a raccoon. Indeed, we vowed, it was a raccoon. There was definitely, through some inexplicable circumstance, a wild raccoon in the bedroom closet. My father entered the closet armed with a broom and came out holding the trophy by its tail. It was a mouse, about the size of a couple of cotton balls glued together.

"The raccoon is still in the closet, Dewey," she said firmly.

She was an awful snob. There was a couple in town who were bakers. They savored all year their annual spring trip to Atlanta to hear the Metropolitan Opera. Lucy thought it unseemly for mere bakers to go to the opera, and she dismissed them loftily as putting on airs.

She considered it a disgrace for a woman to work unless "something happened" to her husband. Even if a woman worked under those circumstances, she thought it a disgrace to her husband's memory that the widow had not been left well fixed enough to stay home and play bridge.

She never knew what to make of me and the newspaper business. It simply baffled her. She was not discouraging. She was simply not interested, and that was not very encouraging.

We operated in different arenas with different sets of expectations and tools—or were they weapons? She once said, almost wistfully, that she thought I was closer to my children than we had been to one another when I was growing up.

I must wistfully agree.

Her last years were sad. It is an old story. There was a fall, a broken hip. She never recovered. The mighty will that should have helped did not fail her, but it did not serve her well. When it came up against the fact of pain and frailty and dependency, there was simply a standoff—and no winners.

She was still defiant. She once slung a breakfast tray at an attending physician. Later, his wife told a stranger that Lucy Dye was the meanest white woman in Manatee County.

I don't know if that made her the meanest woman in Manatee County, or the second meanest.

Anyway, the woman to whom the physician's wife made this observation turned out to be my sister.

The speaker was mortified.

Serves her right, huh?

What do any of us know about the loss of power until we have lost it?

I wish I had known then what I know now.

And don't we always?

Toward the end of her life, Lucy was in a coma for a month. There was no reason to expect that she would recover. I called every few days to speak with her nurse. There was never a change in her condition, except that she grew gradually weaker.

Then, one day I called and the nurse asked if I would like to speak to Lucy.

"Hi, baby," she said. "When are you coming down?"

Just like that.

It was like hearing a voice from the dead, a voice I had never expected to hear again. I cried for an hour after we hung up, in neither joy nor sorrow. Simply in awe. She was back. Where had she been? How had she done it?

Will.

Sheer will.

She got her own way one more time.

I dream about her every now and then. Sometimes, in my dream, I walk down the upstairs hallway to her bedroom and knock on the door, to tell her I'm home, like I used to do when I was a schoolgirl. Except I am not a schoolgirl in my dream and she is old and I am aware that she is sick. But, when I go into her room, she is up and about and strong. The walker is in the room, but she does not need it anymore.

"Mother, you're better," I say. "You're so strong."

"Yes," she says. "I'm going to be all right now."

It takes no particular gift to interpret that dream. Nor this one, either, though its setting is odd as only dreamscapes can be.

In it, we are sitting side-by-side in the open trunk of her green Cadillac. We are swinging our legs back and forth over the bumper like a couple of kids sitting on the edge of a dock. The feeling is happy.

She says something that I do not hear, but I hear my reply.

"Yes, Mother. I love you. But I'm not ready to deal with you yet."

But, of course, the sooner the better.

Conventional wisdom is that we have to forgive our parents to get free of them and get on with our lives. There's an alternative notion going the rounds that it's unnecessary to forgive anyone who's been absolutely toxic.

I dunno.

It sounds like buzztalk to me: Forgive. Withhold forgiveness.

I just want to see what happened, what really happened. I'll settle for that.

Ernest Hemingway closes *Death in the Afternoon* with these words: "Let those who want to save the world if you can get to see it clear and as a whole."

How else is the world saved, except that we see it clear and as a whole?

5

A little piece of the world is ours to save, to see clearly and as a whole, to fix, to change the past.

But we've got to connect the dots.

A few weeks after my husband's death I dreamed that we danced together. He wore a faded brown plaid shirt and corduroy slacks, baggy, forest green, I think. We didn't say anything to one another. I could feel the texture of the shirt, the warmth of his hands, his cheek. The place where we danced seemed to be our living room, yet it was not our living room, or at least it did not remain the living room. It was a mysterious, expanding, retreating, shadowed space that felt limitless, intimate.

The song was "Evergreen": "Spirits rise and the dance is unrehearsed . . ."

I knew the dream would come, though it came sooner than I expected. I knew that the dream was waiting for me because I had had the dream before, after my father's death. The plot and the setting of the first dream were different, but I am certain it is the same dream—the structure and the purpose do not vary.

In the dream about my father, I am standing in the doorway of the house where I grew up. A car pulls into the driveway and my parents get out. My mother goes on about her errand, but my father walks across the lawn to the sidewalk in front of the house and waits there.

I push open the screen door and run out of the house to my father. He hugs me. That's all. He says nothing. I say nothing. He holds me for a moment. I breathe the faint scent of shaving soap, good tobacco. The embrace is made of his abiding, sweet strength. His cheek is against mine; his arms around me are warm.

The dream has an added, interesting element. In it, I know that it is up to me to go to him, to make myself known to him. I know that he will not see me unless I choose. It is my prerogative, the prerogative of the living. That is the rule. Who made the rule? I suppose I did. It's my dream. But where did it come from? Movies? Ghost stories? Some dark place behind a rusted gate in the mind at the end of a path so overgrown that we have all but forgotten it?

I'm a child of my own time, educated in science, technically astute. I know that dreams are based in electrical activity, regular surges of power that agitate random memories, information, anxieties into brief vignettes that make little sense in the light of day, if we remember them at all.

Right.

But every now and then . . .

The dreams of the dance and of my father on the walk were more than random jolts along my neuron paths. They were vivid, intense, concrete, textural.

Brown plaid. Soft flannel. The sound of music. The scent of tobacco.

Most pervasive of all, in both dreams, the element of warmth. Flesh that is warm is alive.

Either I programmed the dreams, or I did not, but whoever put those dreams together selected the detail that says life. And, note this, threw in for good measure "Evergreen."

Evergreen.

Could the message be clearer?

Look, some deep and profound process says, they are not dead. They are warm. They are alive.

*   *   *

The American Association of Retired People, several years ago, conducted a study of reports by widows and widowers of apparently supernatural contact with their dead spouses. Visitations. A sense of the presence of the departed. Little signs and wonders around the house.

Once upon a time the subject was taboo. Nobody talked about it publicly lest he—or, more likely, she—be thought demented, pushed over the edge by grief. But people talk about all kinds of things today—indeed, what don't we talk about?—and once the closet door cracked on the great beyond, the spirits came tumbling out. About half the people participating in the AARP study reported experiencing some sort of paranormal phenomenon after a spouse's death.

I don't know whether my dream qualifies. I think it was extraordinary, but probably not beyond the realm of this world. I think the dream was me, tending to myself in some deep way that I do not understand, nor do I need to understand.

I needed the message.

Apparently most of us need the message, or we would not have come up with so many destinations for the souls of the dead. In every time and every place, every culture has had its vision of paradise.

My vision is neither specific nor consistent.

But I do believe that the souls of the righteous are with God, in whatever way that they are supposed to be with Him.

The Hebrew prayer book says that in life nor death can we go where God is not and that where God is, all is well.

In the Gospel according to Luke, there is a concise argument that runs thus: God is the god of Abraham, the god of Isaac, and the god of Jacob, and, since God is not the god of the dead, but of the living, Abraham, Isaac, and Jacob are not dead.

". . . for all live unto him."

Is the belief a comfort? Would the work of grief have been more difficult without it?

I think so.

I am not pious, but I am a believer, I don't always believe much, but I always believe something. I've kept up a conversation with God. When I needed to hear something, I did.

The feeling was that there is a center, a place to stand that cannot be shaken. I don't know what to call that certainty but faith, or to whom to attribute it but God.

My husband was a Jew.

He wasn't particularly pious either, and his idea of an adequate funeral, so far as I know, was a plain pine box and someone in a yarmulke to read Psalm 23.

Well, Rabbi Gary Perras had other ideas.

The plain pine box and the Psalm were OK. Beyond those points, we had to negotiate just about every detail of the ceremony. Sounds heartless, huh? A man of God quarreling with a bereaved widow over her husband's funeral? But it didn't work that way.

On the contrary, the rabbi's profound determination that tradition would be served, that Henry would have his birthright, grew to be a comfort, a spiritual education. He explained each point as we went through the process. Do this, and you will feel thus.

Consider the matter of the shroud. He must be buried in a shroud, the rabbi declared. Nothing else would do. A shroud. Period. So what's wrong with a blue suit? When it came right down to it, I wasn't even altogether certain what a shroud was. I thought it was more or less like a choir robe, but a friend said he thought it might be more like a sack, a sort of linen body bag that was pulled over the face of the deceased, gathered and tied at the top of the head.

Not to worry, said the rabbi. Would he bury anyone in a sack? The choir robe was closer, he assured me. The reason for the shroud, he said, is that it is not like anything we wear in life. It's the dress of the dead, not the living. The purpose of the shroud, the plain coffin, of each detail was to help the living face death in a clear, clean way, without any cosmetic touch to give false illusion. The purpose was to treat the earthly remains of the person with dignity while enforcing the final recognition that the spirit of the person no longer dwelt in that flesh.

I was persuaded.

Henry was buried in a shroud and in the tallith and yarmulke given to him by his grandfather at his bar mitzvah in 1931. He looked holy, beyond us. We saw that he belonged to God before he belonged to us and belonged to him again.

Everything that the rabbi had told us that we would feel if he were buried according to the Law rather than after the manner of some mild, comfortable, modern compromise with eternity came true in that awesome moment when we saw him for a moment before the casket was closed. Moments do not come more awesome.

The eternal God is thy refuge and underneath are the everlasting arms . . .

The words came into my mind as precisely as if they had been spoken. They came unbidden, charged with power to define a certainty that I could not have named without those words.

Just before we left the cemetery, I looked back once more and saw a dear friend—an Episcopal priest—working beside that remarkable young rabbi to close the grave. This last practical service was not left to a crew of hired hands and their backhoe but was done in steady, heartbeat rhythm by men who did it to honor the man they buried and would not leave among strangers.

The everlasting arms.

6

I went home for Christmas in 1959, on the train, from Jacksonville to Bradenton. I came back late on a bleak, cold, sunless afternoon. The sky and the air and the clouds were the same pale, tarnished shade of silver-gray. I stood in the space at the end of the car as we rolled into the outskirts of Jacksonville, leaning my forehead on the cold glass at the top of the door, looking at the city.

The trees were bare. A fitful wind tugged smoke from the chimneys of small, shabby houses.

I loved the look of it.

It looked like a real city, with a tough side, and that's something I've always liked about it since the first time I saw it. I was a high-school junior, an editor of my school paper, in Jacksonville for a state conference of student journalists.

My roommate was a longtime chum, Jo Ann Anderson, a Baptist preacher's daughter. We were quartered in the George Washington Hotel, a classic, world-weary, Bogey-movie kind of a place with slow ceiling fans and dark polished wood, a hotel where high-school kids went to their junior-senior proms and politicians stashed their whores and old couples celebrated their golden anniversaries and young naval aviators and their brides spent their wedding nights.

You could get anything you wanted at the George Washington Hotel, strike any deal, order the best KC steak east of the Mississippi, or have a serious drink in a serious bar.

Before it was torn down to make room for a parking lot, they auctioned off the George Washington's furnishings. People came by the hordes and carried memories out of that place by the ton, prom nights and hot dates crystallized into the shape of a lamp or a handful of monogrammed crockery. Talk about transmogrification . . .

But that was a long time later.

The journalism conference was, I suppose, in 1952 or 1953. Anybody who would have said then that the George Washington Hotel would one day be hauled away to the brickyard to make room for a parking lot would have been hauled off in a straitjacket. It was an institution where the city did a lot of business. Jacksonville was a wide-open town then, and you could buy anything, fix anything, if the price was right.

A whore set up shop a few doors down the hall from the room that Jo Ann and I shared. She had a line of clients down that hall, sailors mostly, standing patiently, waiting their turn, talking dirty.

Love for sale. Yeah.

Jo Ann and I were fascinated, natch. The closest we had ever come to anything like this was a steamy passage in a copy of *The Amboy Dukes* hidden in the Andersons' attic. Obviously, that wasn't very close.

Each room had two doors, an inner, solid one and an outer door made with louvered shutters, a sort of tropical touch, to allow for privacy and air circulation.

Ideal.

We turned off the light and opened our inner door. We could not see anything through the slats, not really. So we shoved a dressing-table stool into the tiny entrance foyer and spent most of the night balanced there, gazing eagerly at a parade of shoes that shuffled down the hall. That's all we saw—shoes and a few inches of trousers, most of which seemed to belong to uniforms.

The next morning Jo Ann unlocked the door and stepped out into the hall, heading for breakfast. She jumped back into the room and slammed the door.

"She's there! I saw her! Waiting for the elevator!"

"How do you *know*?" I demanded, scrambling past my roommate to shove the door open an inch or two—only in time to see the elevator doors slide shut. "How could you tell?"

"She looked cheap—and she was carrying a hatbox."

So, there you are—luggage tells.

The wheels groaned and squealed against the steel rail as we backed into the station. A few drops of rain slid down the grimy glass. Raw cold oozed into the car like the odor of the pulp mills that hung over the north side when the wind was right or wrong or no matter what the wind did.

I marked it in my mind that I was almost home. When had the transfer of roots from one soil to another taken place? I had not known it had happened until I came back to Jacksonville that December afternoon and thought, *I'm home.*

I saw Henry, a new friend and neighbor, not yet a lover, though the thought had crossed my mind, waiting for me on the platform. The collar of his trench coat was turned up, the brim of his hat pulled down. He had a cigarette. He was grinning at me. Oh yes.

The platform was darkening and noisy—the clash of the big iron-clad wood wheels of the tall baggage carts against rough concrete—and steam leaked from under the cars.

Here's looking at you, kid.

We learn the plot long before we recognize the players. There are spaces inside our heads, our hearts, our imaginations that we spend our lives trying to fill, stories that we keep trying to finish.

I choose the metaphor of a narrative because I think it is possible to live much of real life as if it were fiction, to go along living out situations, dealing with people as if they were our own inventions. Unrecognized, it can be destructive. On the other hand, it's a handy way to understand what is happening to us, to illuminate raw material, give it a certain shape and purpose.

The pattern and the image.

Fiction interprets information, helps us to understand what we're looking for, provides structure for random experience. We've got pictures in our heads. When we see them made flesh, we know it means something; we know that something has come true.

Fiction sets us up, helps to provide plot outlines for our own lives—cosmic Cliffs Notes.

Here's looking at you, kid.

The first time I saw Paris, I came to find the city in my head, the city shaped from books and movies. I came to see landmarks, to visit Napoleon's tomb and Eiffel's tower, the Arc de Triomphe and Mona Lisa.

I came to Paris with other people's language and experiences and expectations in my head. Other people's ideas were all I had to define what was happening to me. I had the Lost Generation and the Left Bank in my head. I had Piaf and a lot of Hemingway in my head. Of course, I found what I was looking for, and I created a new city, my private memoir.

I've always wanted to write about Paris, to work those few days during the summer of 1956 into something—a spare, evocative novel, I suppose—in which all of us are transformed into more interesting people, people with *destinies* like Rick and Ilsa in the winter of 1941.

He says to her, during the bitter time in Casablanca, before he knows the truth about Victor Lazlow: "How long was it we had, honey?"

And she says, "I didn't count the days."

And he says, "Well, I did. Every one of them."

I did, too.

July 31.

August 4.

August 5.

August 6.

August 7.

The story begins in Rome.

I'm on the fifties version of the Grand Tour—a couple of weeks plowing back and forth across the Atlantic on cut-rate student liners, the last voyages of the converted troop transports. We visited nine countries between voyages, twenty or so college girls and two harried chaperones loading on and off buses through the great cities and a few forgotten villages of Europe.

Rome. July 31, 1956. We have been to visit St. Peter's and the Vatican. We have seen the Via Appia and the catacombs. We have returned to the Esperia Hotel and dined on pasta and baked chicken and the night is ours, unscheduled.

I'm traveling with my chum Shirley Granade. Everyone thinks we are sisters because we look alike. Even our luggage looks alike—Wing—hers is red plaid, mine blue plaid, both with little sterling silver nameplates.

See? Luggage tells.

We decide to go for a walk, to find a café. I don't know whether we actually *found* cafés or sort of scouted them out from the sidewalk, yearning to become part of the scene, afraid to join it, our shyness rooted in youth and inexperience, small-town southern girls playing an awkward and unconvincing game of sophistication, collecting impressions of sidewalk cafés the way we took photographs of famous landmarks and acquired Belgian lace and Florentine leather.

We left the hotel and turned up the Via Nazionale.

We paused at a little Anglican church to visit a garden tucked away behind it. When we came out of the garden, two boys, Italian boys in sailor suits, approached us. Good-looking boys. They flirted outrageously, and we demurred flirtatiously and told them that in America sailors were not always nice boys.

What can I tell you? That was the way we talked in the fifties. Furthermore, we knew what we meant. We knew what a nice boy was, and what a nice girl was. The rules were elaborate—all underpinned by the Great Commandment: no penetration—and there were ways around them.

An old woman at the corner sold pink carnations from a big basket, and the boys bought one for each of us.

"We are nice boys," they said, and after a minute or two we began walking up the Via Nazionale together, toward a wide, bright plaza where a fountain was pouring rivers over a fanciful baroque landscape of nymphs and cherubs and what all, polished by centuries, oceans of water sliding, dancing, splashing over the marble.

Pino was tall, broad-shouldered. He had curly brown hair with an unruly lock that fell across his forehead. He had warm dark eyes, the face of an Etruscan warrior from an ancient frieze, a square jaw and a strong, straight nose, good hands, grace, enthusiasm, a wonderful smile and a cheerful spirit. He smelled like Ivory soap.

We sat for a long time in the big café on the square. Twilight turned to dark, and we drank coffee and smoked cigarettes and exchanged information.

After a while we decided to take a walk.

We walked for hours.

There was a moon and the soft, warm night was around us like a cocoon and it felt like we had the city to ourselves. It is a fact that Rome, like the rest of the world, was less crowded, less chaotic, less dangerous thirty-five years ago than it is today. It cannot be true that the city, once we were away from the bright square and its cafés, was deserted except for the four of us.

But that's how I remember it.

We came to the Colosseum. No one was there, no guard to tell us that we could not go in, so we did, our way lit only by moonlight. It is a ruin and the floor of the arena is gone, but, dimly, we could see the outlines of the tunnels that honeycombed the cellar beneath the field of battle and martyrdom, where wild animals were contained, the chariots and the horses housed, where the gladiators and the Christians waited. You'd think a place like that would be haunted, would all but howl with its ancient horrors. Not that night.

We wandered through it for awhile, and then we found private shadows.

Walking back to the hotel, we sang "Arrivaderci, Roma" and "That's Amore" and "Love Is a Many-Splendored Thing." It was like living in a movie about a boy and a girl who meet on the girl's last night in Rome and fall madly in love and cannot bear to part.

The boys promised that they would meet us in Paris.

The next morning, we were on the bus headed for the railroad station by seven-thirty.

We took the train as far as San Remo, and all day we talked about them and we wondered. Would we see them again? We drank vinegary red wine purchased from a cart in one of the stations we passed through, and we ate bread and slices of salami, and we peeled oranges with our fingernails and we talked about them. From San Remo we continued by coach, and we talked about them. When we checked into our hotel in Nice at midnight, we were still talking about them.

We spent two days in Nice, the first set aside for seeing the Riviera sights, the second for hanging out. I have a single indelible memory of Nice. It is of gazing idly from our hotel window, watching a waiter in the café across the street go to the gutter to slosh his rag around in the effluent, wring it out, and go back to wiping off the tables.

We took an overnight express train to Paris. I have a single indelible memory of that train ride. I remember the unfamiliar, exquisite clutch of the thought that I would die if I did not see Pino again. It was simple as that—I would die if I did not see him again.

They hauled us around the city all day, down the Champs Élysées, up Montmartre, past the Eiffel Tower, back and forth across the Seine. That night they marched us off to the opera to see *Tosca*. And when we finally turned back toward the hotel, footsore and dizzy with weariness and culture, Pino and his friend, Nello, saw us coming, way down the Rue de Rivoli, and they shouted and began to run to us and we ran to them and there we were, embracing under Paris skies.

Yes!

Love is a many-splendored thing.

So.

We walked.

I can feel our feet crunching through the gravel in the Tuileries, see us on the Champs Élysées, noticing only when it was time to leave that we had spent an hour in the Colosseum Café and taking the coincidence for a sign and wonder. It was all sign and wonder, all sign and wonder.

I can feel the damp, cool air along the *quai* beside the river, hear the water whisper, slide past us, see the dark that almost covered us and the light from the streets that kept us from the dark. I can feel the texture of Pino's cotton shirt against my cheek.

I can feel the heat.

> *How sad and bad and mad it was—*
> *But then, how it was sweet!*

Oh yes, Mr. Browning. How it was sweet . . .

Paris, summer 1980. Twilight. I am leaning on the rail of Pont Royal, looking down at the same *quai*.

"I know what you're thinking about," my daughter says.

I don't want to leave the place. I can feel us there, almost see us in the twilight. The memory is all but made flesh. It is one of those times when you can believe that everything that has ever happened goes on happening forever, leaving traces, images, echoes in layer upon layer of sensory information that can be retrieved by memory and imagination when you push the right key, the key that creates experience as playback, processed and just a little fuzzy around the edges.

I hadn't expected the memory of the first time I saw Paris to be so strong. I had expected only to play with it.

"Hey, remember who you came with, kid," my husband says playfully. Is he jealous? There's a fine fancy. Yeah. Maybe.

We walk across the bridge, through the Tuileries.

Our feet crunch in the gravel.

The Hotel Saint-Simon, at 16 Rue de Saint-Simon, is un-assuming and pleasant, a private place with a small cob-blestone courtyard and a cozy lounge where one may have a drink or, in the morning, a basket of croissants, still hot from the bakery. A narrow flight of stairs just off the court-yard twists to our rooms. We have a small bedroom, a bath, a tiny room off the bath with a desk and a narrow bed for our daughter.

After our daughter is asleep, we make love, and after Henry is asleep, I go into the bath and balance on the edge of the little tub on its cast-iron cat's feet and I smoke a cigarette and cry. With rampant nostalgia. I feel Paris all around me in the night and I feel my husband and our daughter in the rooms beside me and I feel Pino and Ann a few blocks away, in a dark place on the *quai* with the Seine whispering past them in the night.

I see them negotiating for tomatoes and sausage and bread and cheese and wine at Les Halles for the picnic in the Bois de Boulougne and the little chairs we rented from the old man in the Bois and the night we went dancing in the garden of a restaurant in Montmartre. I remember every day. I remember saying goodbye, and knowing that I would never say goodbye.

Otherwise, why am I sitting on the edge of the bathtub crying?

I have a sense that, if I went early in the morning to the Bois de Boulougne, I would find him there, in the mist, waiting for me. Foolish? Sure. But aren't we there? Shirley is forever spilling wine on her new blouse. The white waxed wrapping paper is spread over the extra chair holding the bright tomatoes and the cheese and bread we sliced with the little pocket knife I still run across every now and then in unexpected places.

7

I suppose that second chances are always unexpected.

We see life as something like Robert Frost's yellow woods, where two roads diverge and the traveler cannot choose both:

> *I shall be telling this with a sigh*
> *Somewhere ages and ages hence:*
> *Two roads diverged in a wood, and I—*
> *I took the one less traveled by,*
> *And that has made all the difference.*

Well . . . yes.

It's true.

But sometimes the path we do not choose has a way of running along beside the way we go and then meandering in another direction and then, suddenly, turning back to cross our path again ages and ages hence in the most unexpected ways.

I went to college at Florida State University in Tallahassee.

Nineteen fifty-four to 1958. Sweet times. The last of our national innocence. Maybe. We like to think so, anyway.

But that's another path to explore.

This path leads to a canopy road.

A college chum, Leslie Lanier, and I discovered that we shared a passion for back roads, backwoods and country churches, crossroads stores. She had grown up in Tall-ahassee and knew her way around the local woods. On week-ends we set out to explore.

The state line that divides Florida from Georgia a few miles north of Tallahassee is more or less a technicality in that neck of the woods. The land is divided by its character rather than marks on a surveyor's chart. Tallahassee is in the plantation belt that spills down from Georgia.

A unique system of old roads—the canopy roads—wander through the plantation country, tying it together like twine wound every which way around and around a package of rolling hills and tangled woods. The system survives, but it is less intact today than in 1958. The roads run through prime real estate nowadays, rather than the boonies.

Anyway . . .

The roads ran through hundreds of thousands of acres of woodland and plantation lands that were, and remain, pri-marily hunting preserves, country retreats for the rich and famous—Ike and Mamie and the Duke and Duchess of Windsor were regulars on fifties guestlists.

A country road becomes a canopy road when the trees, generally oaks, that crowd to the edge of the narrow right of way spread their branches enough to meet overhead. Orig-inally, the roads were dirt trails that wore deeper over the years into something like gullies, dry creek beds. At places, driving a canopy road is like driving through a tunnel be-cause of the overhanging trees trailing moss and the heavy brush pushing in along the sides of the winding roads.

The roads are reminiscent of the Natchez Trace, the path between Natchez, Mississippi, and Nashville, Tennessee, that was used during the early nineteenth century by traders who floated their goods south on the Mississippi River on barges and then walked home up the wide path that eventually was cut so deep into the earth that traces of it are easily seen to this day.

Around Tallahassee, miles of the canopy roads seem literally scooped out of red clay. Tree roots hang from the embankment on each side of the road. Above, vines are tangled in an intricate web.

The woods are thick, dark, mysterious. Primal.

Sometimes the light falls through the trees like light through the stained-glass windows of an old cathedral. It has that same golden cast to it, and dust slowly dances through the shafts of light.

But more often the woods call to another instinct. These are Tarzan woods. Wild Indian woods.

Well, why not? These roads were Apalachee Indian trails long, long ago, and later, they were links between the Spanish missions in North Florida. The English from colonial Georgia put the Spanish missions out of business, and the Civil War put King Cotton in his grave, and the plantations were bought up by rich people from the north who turned them into winter retreats and hunting preserves.

And so they remain.

The plantations are a survival.

The plantation people still ride to the hounds, wear pink coats, blow the hunter's horn, stage elaborate hunt breakfasts, get the dogs blessed at the parish church before they let them loose.

Who blesses the fox? Who blesses the vixen and her brood?

People who know their way around the countryside can spot the little dirt roads that lead off the canopy roads through the woods to the old churches and burial yards and tiny settlements hidden out of sight and knowledge of most passersby.

Leslie knew her way around the woods.

We swam in sinkholes, dealt with bootleggers, visited a half-dozen old meeting houses. Our favorite was Pisgah, a sweet little Methodist church north of Tallahassee, off the Centerville Road. A colony of the dead clustered around its peeling clapboard flanks and we wandered among them, reading Sara Teasdale:

When I am dead and over me bright April
Shakes out her rain-drenched hair,
Though you should lean above me broken-
hearted,
I shall not care. . . .

We noted the sad epitaphs that marked old events of life and death, long forgotten except for an occasional descendant adding names and dates to a genealogy chart, or a college girl spinning epics from a few minor clues.

I wrote a poem: "Pisgah." I don't have it anymore.

My creative writing teacher said that it was good, that something about it—tone? subject?—reminded him of Edna St. Vincent Millay's "Renascence." Later, he decided that he had been more enthusiastic about the poem than it warranted. Later still, in the year after I graduated, he killed himself. The acts—reassessing the poem and killing himself—had nothing to do with one another.

He dedicated a story to me once, an overcast, intense story about a child evangelist. I had put him onto the story, telling him about a roadside tabernacle halfway between Tallahassee and Alligator Point where a nine-year-old boy was running a revival meeting. The odd child traveled with his widowed mama in a big rattling wheezing old Buick, living, between covered-dish fried chicken and snap beans, on Sunbeam bread and bologna sandwiches, and he reaped a mighty harvest of souls for the Lord with his scary, high-strung preaching. Jim went out to the tabernacle to see for himself and made a story out of it, a carefully joined piece of work with all its elegantly turned symbols in place, a story with the bones on the outside, the flesh within.

That was the way it was done in the fifties, after all.

Moby Dick was really death, right? He's no whale, he's death, or good, or evil, or God, with his eye on Ahab, who is no sea captain but Man with the courage of the angels or the pride of Satan, who strikes at God or death—and hits a whale.

Well, Billy Budd is a Christ figure, that much is clear.

But what about the strange little boy on the rocking horse in "The Rocking-Horse Winner"? I was supposed to understand that one. Jim handed me D. H. Lawrence's story one blustery winter afternoon, saying that I would certainly see to the heart of it. Of all of us in the creative writing seminar, he knew that I was the one who would understand it. But I didn't. And the poem that seemed at first to be "Renascence" turned out not to be "Renascence" after all, but rather the sentimental sighing and self-conscious craft and imperfect vision of a college girl, something that now I've misplaced. I would not have thrown it away. It must be somewhere, retreating into the dark at the top of the closet, like a shard in an old campsite, settling deeper and deeper into the earth where the path used to be, just beyond the black gritty circle under the detritus where the clay is forever changed because we built our campfire there, one night, and got right into the center of the universe from wondering where to find it, and then we moved on and lost the place.

No matter.

Can you imagine that we ever cared how to get to the center of the universe?

But I would like to read the poem again.

Jim's wife was thin and dark and watchful. Pretty and sad, with the look of the thin and dark and watchful Modigliani women in the paintings that we bought prints of and hung in our first apartments, along with the Toulouse-Lautrec posters and the reproductions on canvas of the guitar player from Picasso's Blue Period. I almost knew then that her life showed in her face. I did not quite know, but I almost knew. Someone told me that the way it happened was that she went home from work to see about him one morning when he did not answer the telephone and she found him dead. She must have gone to find him already fearing what she would find, or she would not have gone at all, would simply have tried the number again later. She must have gone to find him already knowing what she would find.

He was a Virginian and an Episcopalian and a good writer and a good teacher and he wore vintage tweed with leather patches on the elbows and he had two little boys and his wife with dark, watchful Modigliani eyes that saw into his non-future and loved him desperately and very much, which are not necessarily the same, though not enough to save his life because there was not enough for that. It was not love he lacked for, but hope or confidence or something I cannot call by name.

Oh, there was more in that poem than either of us ever knew. I wonder how it reads, these ages and ages hence.

I did not know that there was anything there at all until I began the ramble about the canopy roads and that took me back to Pisgah and that narrow road diverged into another place entirely.

8

There is a notion among some North American Indian nations that certain people, people with strong medicine, the right magic, can shift their shape, that a man might become an alligator or a panther if he knows the words to say. The idea, obviously, isn't strictly native to North America. There are versions of shape-shifting in most cultures. Consider the werewolf, the vampire, and angels and aliens that we entertain unaware. We deal with creatures of light and darkness who are in disguise for reasons of their own, to seduce us into their darkness, to lead us to their light.

It's the same with second chances. They don't come again in their original shape. They come in disguise, and it is up to us to recognize them.

From the time I was a little child, I wanted to grow up to be a foreign correspondent, preferably a war correspondent.

My first hero was the World War II Scripps-Howard columnist Ernie Pyle. A little later, Marguerite Higgins, battling military men who wanted her barred from covering combat in Korea because she was a woman, was a shining star in my personal constellation of guides, heroes, role models, and such. The words *International Herald-Tribune* trigger sweet longings in my soul to this day.

But I didn't grow up to be a foreign correspondent. No Paris. No London. I didn't even make it over the state line.

Unexpected, then, that I walked into my office at the *Florida Times-Union* one morning and Sarah Wood, head of the features department, said she had a notion that it would be interesting to switch features columnists with the Murmansk-Polar region edition of *Pravda*. For a month or three months or even six months, I could cover Jacksonville's sister city in the Soviet Union, two hundred miles above the Arctic Circle, just as I cover Jacksonville. Keep up with the arts, look for the offbeat, get to know the people. Like that. Was I game? Why not? I agreed as blithely as Prissie's offer to help Scarlett with birthin' Miss Melanie's baby in *Gone with the Wind.*

It did not happen exactly as we imagined it, but it happened.

The day I packed for the flight to Moscow, Leningrad, Murmansk, it struck me that I had grown up to be a foreign correspondent after all. It took fifty years instead of twenty-five, but it happened. I had another shot, a second chance at an old dream.

A few months after I moved to Jacksonville, I was up to my old trick of following country roads to see where they lead and one of them led to a little church—St. Margaret's Church, a chapel built in the nineteenth century for the Hibernia plantation. Suburbia is lapping at its foundations now, but when I first saw it thirty years ago, the little church was deep in the woods, forgotten by most of the world, a Brigadoon of a church, pretty, pretty as a picture, board and batten weathered silver gray, Virginia creeper climbing one wall, inching up onto the roof where old cedar shakes were velvety with soft moss.

What a spot for a wedding, I said to myself.

A few months later I was married—by a justice of the peace in his barber shop in Kingsland, Georgia. We had to pause mid-vows to let a freight train pass so that we could hear what we were promising. No problem. A wedding at St. Margaret's had been a passing fancy, nothing more.

I got intrigued with the history of the place, though. I

wrote a newspaper feature about the chapel and about Margaret Seton Fleming, the mistress of Hibernia plantation. I tried to write a novel based on Margaret's story, but I didn't know how. I had a good title—*The Last Enemy*—but not much grasp of how to create a cast of believable characters in conflict with one another in an authentic, self-contained world. Maybe it's stashed on the same closet shelf with "Pisgah," but I'm not sure I want to read it again. I expect it has its moments, habitable islands poking their heads above sargasso seas where nothing moves along quite as it should.

Perhaps fifteen years after I found St. Margaret's Church at the end of one of my country roads, I had lunch with novelist Eugenia Price. We got together to talk about *St. Simon's Memoir,* her account of finding her special piece of the earth at the edge of the Marshes of Glynn. We talked about that book, and we talked about the next one. What was it to be? The third in the Florida trilogy that already included *Maria* and *Don Juan McQueen.* Both were set in St. Augustine. She was looking for a person from history whose life was dramatic enough to carry a novel and interesting enough for the novelist to endure the long and intimate acquaintance of several years of meticulous research and writing.

I told her that I supposed at least half the people she met had stories for her to write. But why not consider Margaret Seton Fleming?

Eugenia had already considered and passed over Margaret. But she reconsidered, and Margaret Seton Fleming's story was properly told in *Margaret's Story.*

I didn't write the Hibernia novel nor persuade Eugenia Price to write it. But I had a bit part, I suppose, a few key lines to speak.

"Why don't you consider Margaret Seton Fleming . . ."

"Why don't you drive down and take a look at St. Margaret's Church in Hibernia?" I asked my son, Joseph, and his bride-to-be, Julie Sullivan, when they were planning their wedding several years ago. Our parish church was large and modern. They wanted a small, country wedding. St. Margaret's was right for them. It was a beautiful wedding, simple, every detail in place, straight from the heart, sweet-spirited and genuine.

I did not think of it at the time. It was a week before it struck me: I had my wedding at St. Margaret's after all.

So.

The wedding happened.

And the book about Margaret Seton Fleming was written.

Somehow or another, the story of Margaret and Hibernia has got woven into my story as if it had been part of the pattern all along.

Or maybe there's no pattern at all. The mind seeks order as iron filings get themselves lined up north and south in a magnetic field. One of the latest dream theories is that dreams are so often bizarre not because the images hide a deeper, even more bizarre truth, but because the images are made of utterly random and chaotic discharges of energy from the brain stem. In other words, the brain is doing the best it can to make some kind of recognizable image and purpose and order where none exists.

Hey, we've all had days like that.

And then there are those moments when you'd swear you can see through the chaos as if it were glass, straight to the pattern, straight to the truth of what really happened, and, simpy from seeing it, you have begun to fix it.

The guest room at Mount St. Scholastica in Atchison, Kansas, looks out over the back of the convent grounds, down a gentle hill past a vineyard and the cut-flower garden. Beyond the vineyard, land has been plowed, and three nuns and a hired man are planting the kitchen garden.

From where I watch, elbows leaning on the windowsill, the gardeners are faceless, shapeless, ageless. All wear straw hats and blue jeans. I know three are nuns only because I met them this morning on their way to begin the garden.

Knowing, I do not miss their arrangement on the landscape. I do not miss the metaphor, the allusion to Millet's *Angelus*. The sentimental picture of the pious peasants at prayer hangs in my head as the cardboard reproduction hung over the upright piano in Aunt Molly's parlor.

I have come to the convent to visit a cousin, Sister Phyllis Dye. I have not seen her in more than forty years—since she was thirteen and I was seven. She lived with us for a while during World War II because her mother was dead and her father was in the Pacific. The last time I saw her she was a Baptist and a head taller than I. Now I am six inches taller than Phyllis, and she is a Benedictine sister. A lot can happen in forty years.

My ideas of convent life are drawn from books and movies. I know better, of course. I know about Vatican II. I know that the convent has been through a period of upheaval, change, self-examination. Still, the early images remain. I've got *A Nun's Story* and *In This House of Brede* and *The Bells of St. Mary's* in my head. I pictured Ingrid Bergman and a handful of sheltered women dedicated to good works. My cousin reminds me more of Huck Finn than Ingrid Bergman and there are 350 sisters at the Mount, two hundred of whom are there year-round.

When I hear that, at the airport in Kansas City, I think of the pound-and-a-half of crab dip and the two pounds of Swiss Melt cookies I have brought to share with the sisters. I feel like the lad who brought two fish and five barley loaves to the feeding of the multitude.

It works out.

After dinner, that first night, a few sisters come to my room to get acquainted. We drink Dr Pepper and Diet Pepsi and munch out on crab dip and cookies.

It's going to be OK, I think. A week in the convent. Kansas. A change of scene. Something different.

"People in Florida must have thought it was kind of strange—spending your vacation in a convent in Kansas," my cousin speculates.

Actually, we are not, when she says this, in Kansas. We have rented a car and crossed the river into Missouri. We're headed east, all the way across the state to Hannibal. We're on a Mark Twain pilgrimage and getting acquainted, catching up on forty years.

We're listening to Willie Nelson and Merle Haggard on the radio and admiring the countryside. She's telling me about what all happened to her after she left us and about entering the convent and about cousins I've never met. I'm telling her about husband, children, job, what all happened to me.

It takes all day to get to Hannibal, and when we do, there's a festival in progress. A rock band is playing downtown and people are peddling T-shirts and barbecued chicken. We eat some chicken and photograph one another in front of Twain's boyhood home, and then we wander across some railroad tracks and look at the Mississippi River.

We find the car again and drive out along the bluffs above the river, past Tom Sawyer's cave. Then we double back and cross over into Illinois, go down to the bank of the river and pick up a couple of clam shells, a few pebbles. We drive past a cornfield, its stalks barely knee-high. My cousin tells me that, in August, if you stand quiet in the middle of a cornfield, you can hear the corn grow.

When we get back to Atchison, we look up Sister Faith to give her a sliver of Tom Sawyer's fence (not the original, but it's the thought that counts) that we picked up for her. She is a poet, and she taught English at Benedictine College for decades, so it seems an appropriate gift.

She is pleased.

Many of the sisters are old now.

The newest part of the convent is a retirement and infirmary annex.

The graying of the order.

When my cousin was a newcomer, part of her class's discipline was to take Q-tips into the lovely old choir chapel and remove the dust speck by speck from each detail of the elaborately carved wood. No more. The choir chapel gets a lick and a promise from the dust rag these days. There are not many young girls coming to the convent now.

Several times, after supper, I join the sisters in the choir chapel for evening prayer. We sit facing each other across the center aisle, and I think how weary they look. They remind me of country women who have worked from dawn tending a large place, a large family. They look plain and enduring.

What I did not understand before I shared the sisters' life was community, at least not in the sense that they create it. I had thought of the convent as the building where they lived while their "real" lives were carried on in their work.

Wrong.

My cousin is a teacher and a librarian. Several years ago, she came home to stay at the Mount, and she now keeps the cut-flower garden and works in the canning kitchen. When she wrote me of this change, I thought: Heaven forbid. I thought: Suppose I had to give up the newspaper business and can tomatoes instead. I thought: She can't really not mind.

But she doesn't. She asked to come home to the Mount, to do quiet, plain work.

The convent bakes its own bread; makes preserves and jellies; cans and freezes and pickles fruits, vegetables. My cousin loves it when a truckload of culls arrives from Kansas City and she and the other sisters who work in the canning kitchen pick out enough good to feed the community.

She loves it best when she has caught, cleaned, and put by enough fish to feed the community. That's a bunch of fish, but my cousin is a great fisherman.

We go fishing one day at the sisters' cottage at a lake a few miles from Atchison. Her pockets are full of pliers and knives and bits of tackle and string. We use worms and lures and she goes about it with quiet, introspective profession-alism. She even takes catfish off the line without losing her dignity. I'd handle a snake as soon as I'd handle a catfish.

I'm fairly put off by the fins on a panfish that I reel in. The desperate, doomed thing flops wildly on the end of the line, the fins along its back rigid as sawteeth.

"I'm scared of it," I call to her shamelessly, hoping she will offer to remove the fish from my line and string it up with the rest of the keepers.

"Offer it up," she replies mildly.

"Offer it up . . ." I repeat. "Sure." She's not a Baptist any-more.

We fry our fish and steam some fresh asparagus and slice strawberries for dessert. We watch the sun set over the lake and then my cousin makes certain that the cottage is scrupulously clean before we leave.

Back at the convent, I follow her through a labyrinth of dark halls to a storage room with a refrigerator, where she stashes her night crawlers.

Nothing is ever wasted at the convent. When the traditional veil and habit became optional, the sisters who chose to wear modern clothes turned in their habits so that the material might be kept to repair the garments of the sisters who chose to dress traditionally. It is mostly the very old nuns who still wear the full habit.

In the dining room I watched the youngest woman—in her first year at the convent—in jeans and plaid blouse as she helped a sister, almost one hundred years old, in the ancient, restraining habit of the Benedictine order. They live in the same world, keep the same rule of life. It is so mysterious to me that I can only turn it over in my mind and wonder.

What brings the girl to the convent? What brought the old nun? I suppose there are as many answers as there are nuns at the Mount. Surely, they bring an instinct to serve God. I suppose that in some the instinct is lofty, in others humble. But, whatever its original shape, it seems to me that, at its best, it is finally shaped by community life into love, into caring for one another in ordinary matters with extraordinary interest.

The day that I left the convent to come home, the sisters whom I had met only a week before gave me gifts—homemade bread, jars of plum and apple butter, a hand-crocheted afghan, a hand-turned cup shaped of Kansas clay.

On the plane I thought about how, on that first day at Mount St. Scholastica, I had recalled the boy who brought five barley loaves and two fishes to a hillside when he went there to hear Jesus teach. Jesus multiplied the gifts and fed five thousand with a few fish, a few loaves of barley bread.

Something like that happened to me at the Mount. I do not mean that Swiss Melt cookies and crab dip were multiplied and reshaped and returned in generous measure under the guise of homemade bread and preserves and an afghan and pottery. Though I suppose that's one way to look at it, too. No, I mean that I brought curiosity and, hidden beneath the curiosity, the unfinished business of Phyllis's unexpected and wrenching departure from our house one midnight about a year after she came to live with us.

It felt as if the Nazis had taken her. It wasn't Nazis. It was an uncle or aunt on the way to Kansas City with room for her in the car, and the decision had been made that she should return to Kansas City to be with her mother's people.

The removal was carried out with brutal efficiency. One night she was there. The next morning she was gone. I don't even remember telling her goodbye.

I just remember, afterwards, wandering around the house and the yard and the neighborhood, looking for her, knowing that she was gone and looking for her anyway. Poor, poor baby. I was seven years old. I didn't know how to deal with the pain and the sense of loss, and no one helped me deal with it, and maybe no one even knew about the pain or knew that I needed help.

I suppose they spied me moping under the hickory nut tree where no grass would grow and we had turned the patch of sand into a battlefield for our lead soldiers. I suppose they thought *she'll get over it.*

And I did. In the long run.

9

In a way.

But what does it mean, to get over something?

Things that happen to us do not go away. We cannot change the past. When we start digging through it, we can hope only to see it more clearly, and thus to change its power to affect the present. Otherwise, there are odd, unfinished patches on the surface that hide something underneath that may be toxic, or may be treasure, but, in either case, is better seen than hidden.

The process is something like unraveling metaphors, metaphors that, in many instances, were made before we had the language or analytical power to understand what was happening. Or perhaps we had the language, but not the heart, or guts, for it. Perhaps something warned us off getting too analytical too soon—dealing with some pieces of the past is like defusing unexploded bombs. It takes will and a steady hand and a guardian angel—and it could still blow up in your face.

The failure of grownups to tend to a grieving, baffled child created unfinished business that eventually developed its own imperative, powerful enough to draw me to the convent in Kansas. If they had done everything right, I suppose that I would not have been left with unfinished business and I could have folded cousin Phyllis away like a baby blanket, stashed in the attic, more or less forgotten.

Things never begin where they seem to begin.

That first trip to Kansas did not begin with the purchase of the ticket, or the decision to go.

It began on the night that Phyllis was taken away.

Several years ago I spent two weeks at Christ Church College in Canterbury as part of a seminar looking at contemporary theology—God in the world today. The seminar was organized by the Christian Organizations and Advisory Trust in association with the Dean and Chapter of Canterbury Cathedral and Christ Church College. It caught my eye for several reasons. It was a chance to spend several weeks in England in a room with a view of Canterbury Cathedral and to meet people who were likely to be compatible and companionable. And I'm interested in the subject—God in the world today. It was a very good way to spend my summer vacation, the ultimate Vacation Bible School.

There were about ninety of us, mostly clergy. We were from nine countries and represented seven denominations. We were an international and ecumenical crew. Our mornings were given to study and lectures and our afternoons were generally our own. There were excursions—a visit to a castle, a day in France, an afternoon at an archaeological dig—and evening entertainment of a rather mild sort.

Ideas were exchanged, friendships flourished, roles were assumed. It did not take us long to turn ninety sundry souls into a temporary community, all pilgrims in one way or another.

What to do on a pilgrimage? We learn from Chaucer only what happens on the way to Canterbury, not what to do once we are there. Perhaps there are rules and people who know them, but I am not one of them. I realize that I will have to make it up as I go along.

It feels right to me to go each day to the cathedral, to look at it, to listen to it, to explore it, to experience it.

There are times when I feel that I am living in those lines from Matthew Arnold's "Dover Beach":

The Sea of Faith
Was once, too, at the full, and round earth's shore
Lay like the folds of a bright girdle furled.
But now I only hear
Its melancholy, long, withdrawing roar,
Retreating, to the breath
Of the night wind, down the vast edges drear
And naked shingles of the world.

In the Middle Ages the sea of faith was at its flood, and England and Europe's great cathedrals were like mighty ships built to sail those deep, well-charted waters. Forever.

Things have changed.

The sea of faith has subsided. We live in a secular age.

Those ancient ships of faith sail a precarious course today.

But they sail.

They do not drift.

They are not dead wrecks cast up on the naked shingles of Dover Beach.

They breathe.

Inside Canterbury there is a sound like the sound of the sea caught in a shell. It is the sound of voices, scores of voices blended and stirred, rising into the great stone vaults of the ceiling, mixed there into an indistinct murmur, the sound of a mountain creek falling over rocks, the sound of surf crashing on a distant beach.

It is a vital, human sound.

Every day an endless parade of twentieth-century pilgrims wanders through the nave, the choir, the undercroft. The building breathes and murmurs with their presence.

Most seem to be secular pilgrims, tourists who come to wonder at the antiquity, the magnificence, the stunning technology wrought by twelfth-century men such as William of Sense and William the Englishman and their bands of stone masons.

Some come to pray.

Some come caught somewhere between those poles—to wonder and to pray, and to wonder that we pray.

The woman does not appear to be eighty-two years old. Her hair is barely gray. Her step is firm and swift. Her blue eyes are bright and clear behind her spectacles.

"I was raised by my mother to put God first, other people second, and myself third," she says, matter-of-factly. You could almost see a little girl's hands threading the Victorian motto into a bit of needlework.

She is the widow of a military officer and lives in Canterbury now to be close to the cathedral. She carries on a personal work among her peers whose steps are less lively, eyes less clear.

"I have older people to tea in the afternoons. They have so little chance to get out. I sew for them. I do their mending because I still sew quite well," she says.

She comes to the cathedral to pray, but she is not annoyed by the tourists who do not.

"Perhaps it is the only way that they come into a church," she says mildly.

She can see the cathedral from the window of her cottage. At night the great structure is flood-lit and floats over the dark town, dream-like, a shining, towered fortress.

"Every night," she tells me, "I look out of my window before I go to bed and I say 'good night' to the cathedral. Odd, I suppose . . ."

Perhaps it is not as odd as it sounds.

When you have lived long enough in sight of one of the great cathedrals, it must cease to be an ancient, lifeless fabric of stone and glass and become a presence.

The Venerable Bede wrote that when Augustine and his band of monks came to Canterbury in 597 to convert pagan Britain, they found a ruined church built by Roman Christians in ancient times. The Saxon cathedral that grew from Augustine's restoration of the Roman church was destroyed by fire in 1067. The history of the present building has been continuous since 1070, and since the end of the fifteenth century it has been more or less in its present form.

History.

All of those centuries seemed translated into people, and

the people translated into the fabric of the cathedral. The effect was not of antiquity, but of immediacy.

Gothic cathedrals are never finished works. They are not static monuments to the achievements and aspirations of another time. They are a process that does not end.

We reinforce with stainless steel work begun with shaped stone, calculate on computers loads and stresses that were once calculated in a master builder's head. We tend, we enhance, we build as they did, with the best that we have. We are heirs, but we are also full partners with those who began the work.

The stained glass at Canterbury dates from the twelfth century. The faces of the old kings and saints and clerics are accurate portraiture, but most of the once-celebrated names are forgotten, execpt to a historian. A twentieth-century window, then, gives pause. It is J. M. Comper's Coronation Window. The lower panel commemorates the coronation of King George VI in 1937. His daughters—Elizabeth and Margaret Rose—are children. The upper panel commemorates the coronation of Queen Elizabeth II in 1953. Prince Charles and Princess Anne are children.

Someday, when they and we are all gone, the window will remain and those faces forever frozen in colored glass will be as remote as the depiction of Henry II at the tomb of St. Thomas in the cathedral's Trinity Chapel.

Becket. It was the murder in 1170 of Thomas Becket by Henry II's knights that brought Canterbury its greatest fame, its greatest prosperity. Becket's tomb, where miracles were claimed by the faithful from all over Christendom, made Canterbury the third—after Jerusalem and Rome—most popular destination of the medieval pilgrim. Their numbers—and gifts—made the cathedral and the little city rich.

Becket, who was appointed archbishop of Canterbury by his boyhood friend King Henry II, died because he used the power of the church to challenge the power of the throne. What may have been no more than a misunderstood remark by Henry—"Who will rid me of this troublesome priest?"—sealed the archbishop's doom. The people made him a martyr, the church made him a saint, the cathedral built a great shrine to hold his bones, Henry VIII destroyed the shrine in 1538 and caused Becket's bones to be scattered to the winds.

I look at the stark, contemporary sculpture that marks the spot of Becket's grisly murder and wonder: What has this to do with us, in the twentieth century?

Nothing. Everything.

It is part of a fabric that stretches beyond the Middle Ages, beyond Canterbury.

Just by the site of Thomas's shattered shrine, behind the high altar of the cathedral, there is a chapel dedicated to the saints and martyrs of our century. There are portraits there of the Reverend Martin Luther King, Jr., of John Kennedy.

Canterbury. Memphis. Dallas. They are all of a piece with something in us that builds and destroys. The murder of men and dreams, the mute, inarticulate making of martyrs by which we cry out against the murder are part of the fabric of the cathedral, of its immediacy, of its presence, its aliveness.

One night, after the cathedral is closed, the group from Christ Church College is taken on a special tour. We are divided into three groups, and men who live all of their lives in intimate contact with the cathedral lead us through its great spaces and its forgotten corners.

They speak of a thousand years of history as if it were a watch in the night. Henry VIII's destruction of Becket's tomb, the Cromwellian fanatics' desecration of the cathedral, Hitler's bombs are all but gathered into a single sentence, intensely spoken.

Our questions, their answers rise through the great, still space of the dim cathedral, and the words are lost in the sound of the sea caught in a shell, a living murmur, as if the building breathes.

We are its breath.

We go into the choir for compline, the ancient order for the last prayers of the day.

Be our light in the darkness, O Lord . . .

Be present, O merciful God, and protect us through the hours of this night . . .

Visit this place, O Lord, and drive far from it all snares of the enemy; let your holy angels dwell with us to preserve us in peace; and let your blessing be upon us always . . .

We walk home through the night.

Behind us, the flood-lit cathedral seems to float, dream-like, over the dark city.

One of our lecturers at the seminar suggests a homework exercise for us. Consider, he suggests, how we came to be at Canterbury. Identify the people who brought us here.

Who brought me to Canterbury?

Almost every day, after lunch, I go down the back lane behind the college. I pass an apple orchard behind a high wall where, one afternoon, I see the Archbishop of Canterbury, in his shirtsleeves, picking apples. Apples? Could that be? In June? Well, there was an orchard. There were fruit trees and the Archbishop of Canterbury was there, in his shirtsleeves, picking fruit, filling a basket with it. He had come down for the day, from London, to spend time in the orchard. Further along the narrow lane, I pass the ruined arches of a medieval monastery where, one morning in a cold mist, we celebrate the Eucharist on an altar that might have served old Druids before it served the monks whose path we followed, and lost, and followed again, all of us together, a communion of saints.

We are surrounded by such clouds of witnesses.

The lane ends at a gate just across from the cathedral grounds. Almost every day I go into the church. I explore a bit and then, finally, I find my place in the choir chapel. It is toward the middle of the farthest row of stalls from the aisle, an inconspicuous place. I sit down, settle down, take a couple of deep breaths and let the question roam free through the great stone vault above me that stirs the sounds of Canterbury into its vital murmur.

Oh, I think of my father and even, fancifully, recall a distant forebear who was the first Quaker in Ireland. Now there's a fellow who would have understood Robert Frost's west-running brook that could trust itself to go by contraries. But mainly I think of Uncle Walter McDonald, the old country preacher who died before I was born.

His name comes to me out of the murmur.

Odd. I never saw the man, but I see him now as the person who brought me to Canterbury Cathedral.

And I brought him to Canterbury, an unexpected companion on an uncharted pilgrimage.

We have come a long, long way from Hopewell.

Back in
the USSR

10

I can't explain how Uncle Walter got to Canterbury.

But I know how Henry Hyman got to Red Square.

He was a natural fellow traveler, so to speak, on that journey to a place I had never expected to see.

The Hotel National is a historic, rather handsome old pile of stone, substantial, poorly lit and overheated, built in 1903. It is an important hotel. Serious business is done there. It's in the center of the city—in fact, it was from a balcony of the Hotel National that Margaret Bourke-White, in 1941, made her stunning photograph of the dark towers of the Kremlin back-lit by German bomb bursts and the searchlights and streams of anti-aircraft tracers of Moscow's defenders.

I get deposited there, by myself, the first night in Moscow because of a mix-up in my travel arrangements from Moscow to Murmansk. The Jacksonville delegation that I am accompanying is taken off to be wined and dined and welcomed to Moscow—and I'm abandoned. I don't care. I don't know why, but I'm high as a kite. I've seldom felt more alive. I'm running on pure energy and it's generating confidence and some kind of I-don't-give-a-damn adrenalin high that feels good and absolutely irresistible. I don't know what's going to happen about my train tickets to Murmansk—I don't care— it'll work out.

I stash my bags in my dark little room and come back downstairs and stand out on the sidewalk in front of the hotel, restless, alert, looking across a wide, busy boulevard at Red Square.

Red Square.

The sight of it, floating across the way, rising out of the darkness, reminds me of the castle at Disney World, a distant piece of scenery from a thousand dramas, not quite real.

Except it's real.

Red Square is not dark, as much of the rest of the city is, as Sheremetyevo Airport was an hour or so ago. It is bathed in light. Even across the wide boulevard that separates me from it, I can tell that, though it's almost ten o'clock, there are people there, lots of people.

I've got to get there.

I can't figure out how to get across the street, and I don't know how to ask. But I explore a little farther away from the door of the National and finally spot an underground pedestrian crossing. I can tell by the hieroglyph of feet descending stairsteps. I descend. It's like a subterranean river of people, swift currents in fur hats and boots and overcoats, flowing between intersections and a metro station, upstream and down. Russians! I recognize my first Russian word on a sign in the underground—it looks like *pectopah*—and I remember from the sprinkle of information I have retained from a conversational Russian class a few weeks before my departure that it means restaurant.

I come out of the tunnel and it's all there—St. Basil's Cathedral, Lenin's tomb, the Kremlin. I feel like Mary Tyler Moore at the beginning of the old series set in Minneapolis-St. Paul—I want to toss my cap in the air. I'm in Moscow! I'm standing in Red Square!

It's not like seeing Times Square or Piccadilly Circus or the Place de la Concorde. Those places all have a hold on our imaginations long before we see them, but not like Red Square. Maybe that's because we expect to see London and Paris. We don't expect to see Moscow, at least I didn't.

The Kremlin isn't Buckingham Palace, where we have been going, in our imaginations, since Christopher Robin went down with Alice. The Kremlin is mystery. It is alien, often sinister. More Eastern than we know. It is power and intrigue and fact and fiction. History and legend. It is Peter the Great and Ivan the Terrible. Tolstoy's Prince Andre and Natasha. Boris Godunov. Napoleon. Tchaikovsky. John Reed and *Ten Days That Shook the World.* Rasputin. Anastasia. Lenin. Stalin. Hitler at the gates. General Georgi Zhukov. Mikhail Gorbachev.

Russia. Holy Russia and Soviet Russia. I stand in Red Square, on the edge of both.

Moscow is a big city—nine million people—but there are few bright lights. Moscow nights can be starry nights. On this one the moon is about three-quarters full. It hangs between the cross on one of the onion domes of St. Basil's and the red star on the Tower Gate of the Kremlin.

The cross, the moon, the red star. It's some kind of sign, a metaphor, a real-life riddle riding in the dark sky.

What does it mean? Who knows? Everybody who writes about the Soviet Union says, at some point, that the land is a great mystery, an enigma. I'm certainly no expert, just one more writer in search of an image to wrap around my version of the mystery, the enigma. I've been in the Soviet Union, at this point, for a couple of hours. Red Square could be a movie set. I'm still inhabiting my own imagination, barely in touch with the real soil and air and people around me.

I wander around for a long time, around the edge of the square and through the center, watching all of us wander around Red Square, watching each other, watching the changing of the guards at Lenin's tomb, watching the occasional limousine that goes in or out the Kremlin gate.

It's a strange feeling, just me, halfway around the world from home.

I wish that my daughter, Elizabeth, were with me. I want so powerfully for her to see this that I almost cry—I think how she would absorb it, how much she would see and understand and connect with everything around her.

And I want Henry to see that I made it.

I remember that question posed by the lecturer in Canterbury: how did I come to be where I am?

How did I come to be here?

Who really brought me to Red Square?

March 8, 1960.

It's my birthday.

Three of us—my roommate and I and our neighbor—celebrate at Le Chateau, a good place in sixty, but eventually pulled down to make way for a condo. It is all 1920s glamour and Spanish tile, a fountain in a courtyard and a legend that a gangster owned the place before it was a restaurant. There is a little dance floor and a wonderful bar. It is on the Atlantic. The ocean rolls up into the light cast across the sand from the floods mounted on the building and then disappears back into the dark, a conjurer's trick.

There is a moon about three-quarters full.

There is a ship on the horizon. We see its silhouette and its navigation lights.

Henry tells my roommate and me that we must not let our horizons remain limited to our schoolgirl vision of the world. He taps lazily at the window, gesturing toward the Atlantic Ocean that rolls onto the floodlit sand out of the darkness and is pulled back into the darkness again. He tells us that ocean touches every shore in the world, and we ought to see some of those beaches, ought to go where the ocean goes and forget where we have always been, what we have always known, what other people expect of us. He says we should think, instead, of how much there is out there in the world for us if we'll go after it.

It could have been a you-only-go-around-once script.

We giggle and think he's drunk. He is, a little. We are, too. I'm twenty-four.

After dinner we walk down to the beach, watch the waves roll into the light and out to the darkness.

He says, *It's all yours, kid—everywhere it goes.*

It feels like we're standing on an edge. There's a March lion of a wind pushing us around and it's got teeth and it tastes of salt.

I love what he says.

I half believe it.

What happens is very different.

Except, almost thirty years later, I am standing in the middle of Red Square, by myself, in the middle of the night, looking at the moon hanging between St. Basil's cross and the Kremlin red star and I am thinking of that birthday celebration at Le Chateau.

So.

Here's looking at you, kid.

11

There are two things that will forever define Russia for me.

One is the train ride from Moscow to Murmansk—long, difficult, total immersion in Russian experience. Unforgettable.

The other is the Easter Eve service that I attended in a Russian Orthodox Church in Moscow—long, difficult, total immersion in Russian experience. Unforgettable.

And I think of the people.

The crowds that packed Russian churches for Easter services in 1988 were indescribable. The numbers are always staggering, but they may have been even greater than in other years because the country was observing the millennium of Russian Christianity—officially noting the one-thousandth anniversary of the conversion of the Ukrainian city of Kiev. It was in Kiev, in 1088, that Emperor Prince Vladimir—later St. Vladimir—ordered his subjects to wade into the Dnieper River to be baptized, and they did.

"Before this time, the people were pagans," said Tamara, an Intourist guide who withheld her last name.

Could Intourist, the official Soviet travel and tourism organization, help to arrange a visit to an Orthodox church for Easter services, I wondered.

"No." She shook her head earnestly. "The church and the state are separate. We are the state. We have no contact with the church. We can tell you where to go, but we cannot provide more. I want to tell you it will be impossible. On this holiday, the people are a mob trying to get in."

Her information was essentially accurate. It did not turn out to be impossible to get in, but thousands of Believers, as Christians are called in the Soviet Union, thousands of Believers who were stolid and solemn and unsmiling as figures in an old, candlesmoke-darkened pastoral landscape were compressed flesh against flesh into the dim, low stone-vaulted, flickering space of an Orthodox sanctuary near Red Square.

The Believers were young and old. I watched a young woman with a little boy perhaps four years old move from icon to icon before the service began. Before each image, she took the child's hand and guided it in the sign of the cross, making the imprint on the boy's body, in his muscles and reflexes, in his mind and and his memory and his heart.

Once, the Russian Orthodox Church was understood to be sustained on a raveling lifeline by the fervent piety of the grandmothers. Official guides pointed out that only the old still believed.

No more.

Young men and women were among the middle-aged and the old who moved eagerly to receive the flame passed from one person to another in that Easter Vigil service that ended with a ritual candlelighting and with cries of "Christ is risen! Christ is truly risen!"

In churches across the Soviet Union, the bells sounded at midnight and the light was passed from hand to hand, and outside the church people who did not go inside—perhaps because they could not get in, or because they feared to go in, or because they were not certain what it was that called them there and did not trust it entirely—lit candles, brushed away the snow, and stuck the candles, with a bit of melted wax, to the stone windowsills. Candles inside, candles without.

I'm not certain of the name of the church where I saw Easter in. It was a half-mile from my hotel, a few hundred yards up a narrow side street from Gorky Street. It was one of thirty working churches in a city of nine million souls.

Long before midnight people began to fill the church. Those who came early brought special bread, cakes, and dyed eggs for blessing. A tall, bearded young priest with a scrubbed look and a shy smile blessed the offerings, dipping a clutch of broom straw into a pot of holy water and shaking it over the bread, the eggs, the people. The water was cool striking our faces.

In deep pockets of his cassock, he had a stash of decorated eggs, which he gave to people as he moved through the church and accepted decorated eggs and sweets that were given to him.

Though not everyone left the church, there was a lull between the early blessing of the eggs and the bread and the beginning of the midnight liturgy. The doors were bolted, and old women mopped the uneven stone floor and polished the brass candle standards that held a thousand slender tapers flickering and burning before the icons that the Russian pious believe have in their material, in the very wood and paint and gold, in their disturbing, otherworldly images of saints and the Virgin and Christ, power, real power, not mere symbol.

The people waiting outside for the church to be prepared for the midnight liturgy began to tap and then to knock and finally to pound at the door for admittance. It was eerie. The sound boomed in the hollow stone space of the church. It was dark, except for a few dim light bulbs and the candlelight. The old women moved silently, single-mindedly through their work of making the church ready for what was to come next, and the people waiting outside in the snowy Moscow night pounded, pounded, pounded for admission.

Finally, the doors were open and people poured into the dim sanctuary. It was quickly full, but more and more and more came. It is literally true that we were packed so tightly together that it was impossible to move. A young man who reminded me of my son and two of his young friends became my partners—I suppose that is an apt word for the connection we formed—for four hours of the service. We stood with a wall on one side of us and the crushing, surging flood of people on the other, forming a sort of mutual defense barricade. Survival worship. It was tricky. If we allowed the crowd to move us away from the wall, and we lost its stability and protection, we were lost. We would be separated and, alone, surely perish. But, if we allowed the crowd to move us into the wall, we would be crushed. This sounds like exaggeration. It is not. At times we actually linked our arms to hold back the crowd from moving us from our place beside the wall. We formed a link between us like children playing a version of the playground game Red Rover. It was scary. If anyone became panicky, I thought, people would undoubtedly be injured, killed, crushed in a stampede of Believers. But no one else seemed alarmed or afraid, so I took my cue from their mood. Besides, I could not leave. I could not move. I could not take a step in any direction, not even a deep breath.

People passed candles intended for individual prayers overhead, from hand to hand, to be lit and placed before the images by the people nearest the icons. When I took a candle from someone's hand and passed it to another hand—to the young man who looked like my son—and watched it move through other hands until it was lit, I thought how strange and sweet and sobering to hold the prayers of a stranger, even for a moment, in our hands.

We are to bear one another's burdens.

I thought of that, of the prayers held in the slender wax tapers that we passed from hand to hand. One another's burdens, praise, despair, faith, unbelief.

I had bought two tapers before the service from an old woman in the back of the church, and I gave one to the young man to pass forward to be lit at an icon of the Virgin, just beyond our reach. There were no prayers, no words, no special intentions that went with it. Instead, there was the feeling that I wanted to trust something that needed no words. I wanted to trust it to us, to all of us, to pass forward and light and set before the ancient image of the mother of Jesus.

Outside, more people stood pressed together in the cold night for the moment when the doors of the church were thrown open and the priests led a procession outside, shouting "Christ is risen!"

The shout was triumphant.

Christ is risen!

Christ is risen, indeed!

A few days earlier the mood of Holy Week had been somber, indeed frightening.

Zagorsk is forty miles north of Moscow.

Between rows of painted houses, the town's dingy side streets and narrow lanes are ankle-deep in mud. The earth oozes under patches of dirty snow. It is spring.

Zagorsk, population fifty thousand, is a historic center of Russian religious life. In 1988 Pimen, Patriarch of Moscow and All Russia, head of the Russian Orthodox Church, still had his seat here at the fourteenth-century monastery of Trinity-St. Sergius. The seat of the patriarch has since moved to Moscow.

But, with or without the patriarch, the monastery is bound to dominate the town as it has for more than six hundred years.

Pilgrims and tourists come to Zagorsk by the thousands. They come on the Intourist buses, explore another world, and leave. But the old women—the legendary old women of the Russian church—are always there.

Good Friday.

The old women sit in a semicircle in an anteroom outside the sanctuary of Trinity Cathedral. They watch pilgrims and tourists move steadily through the anteroom into the sanctuary. Some only watch, faces as expressionless as the flat, even features of a badly executed reproduction of a Byzantine icon. Others pray.

They prostrate themselves on the uneven floor of the cold,

bleak anteroom, weeping, covering the feet of the images of Jesus with tears, with kisses, touching their foreheads to the floor at the feet of the icons over and over and over in a ritual of piety and humility choreographed one thousand years ago.

There is nothing like this in the West's post-Enlightenment version of the faith. There is not this sense of the supernatural, of the passionate intertwining of time and eternity. It is difficult to confront. It is too naked. It is alien. Alien. It is not democratic. In the West, God reigns with the consent of the governed. But the consent of the governed is not necessary in Byzantium. It is not even a consideration. In Holy Russia, the icons themselves are sacred, and their eyes watch, watch, watch, move over the dim sanctuaries as the candlelight moved across the ancient surface of sacred paint, consecrated gold.

Inside the sanctuary some of the women sing. It is eerie. Their voices fill the dark space like the voices of young girls, so that it is difficult to believe that it is the old women who sing. Many of the women approach the relics of St. Sergius, preserved in a silver coffin, and prostrate themselves there, beneath a wall of icons that seems to stretch beyond view in the darkness.

Other women do not move at all in the sanctuary, but rest around the walls, in the semi-darkness. Some literally lie on the floor, motionless, almost heaped together, submerged in piety, floating somewhere beneath the surface of the chants, the candle flame, the prayers, the icons. A shaft of light the color of pewter, a shaft of light that holds motes of dust and the smoky golden breath of candles comes through a narrow window high in the thick wall of the cathedral and holds a woman in it as if she were on stage, lit by a spotlight. She is ancient. She has no legs.

Outside, on the courtyard, a bearded priest speaks, in English, to a group of pilgrims.

"To come to see is one thing," he says. "To come as a pilgrim is another. Follow our ancient practice and prostrate yourselves before the relics of St. Sergius. He is with us here, always, invisibly. Pray to follow him and, God grant, to meet him in the Kingdom of Heaven."

St. Sergius.

Who was he? Who is he? What are his bones in the silver casket that the old women cover with pious kisses?

If I meet him in the Kingdom of Heaven, what will I say? Will he be my brother? That's what the communion of saints teaches me. Well. We'll see. We'll see.

Men and women from the twentieth century follow the priest into the church, where the old women watch and pray.

I am a Believer.

But I have no notion of the world, the spiritual world, inhabited by these women. They frighten me, as if they are specters from a dark folk tale, a tale with roots in every mind.

They put me off.

I stand back from them.

I want their hands and the hands of their children to carry my candle forward to the icon of the Virgin, but I cannot meet their eyes, and if I could, we could not see one another because we are not in the same dimension. Our coordinates do not cross.

Later, on the drive from Zagorsk to Moscow, we pass a convoy of trucks bearing young conscripts for the Red Army from some provincial training station toward Moscow. They look so young. So forlorn. I think, oddly, that I have more in common with them—the young Soviet soldiers—than I have with the old women of Zagorsk.

On Moscow's Maly Vuzovsky Per, on the night of Holy Thursday, a woman approached the Baptist church, tried the door and found it locked.

I watched her from across the street and wondered, melodramatically, if I were the only one who watched. She joined a trickle of people moving down an alley to a side entrance to the church, and I followed her.

It was an hour before services and the church was almost full. A space designed for perhaps one thousand soon held twice that, and perhaps more. We were jammed together, but it did not compare to what I would experience in the Russian Orthodox Church. And we were seated on wooden pews, uncomfortable, oddly designed to bend every joint at the wrong angle, but still seated. Again, old women predominated, but these were not the sanctified sisters of Zagorsk. These old women reminded me of Kate, my Jewish mother-in-law. They had the same faces, the Tartar shape of the eyes, full of craft and curiosity, and the plain, strong features, the scarves tied over hair caught back in a knot—a sort of universal Eastern European bubbe-look.

The men were better dressed. Many wore business suits of reasonable cut and quality. Some of the young people came as close to looking like American kids as any I saw in the Soviet Union in terms of style and demeanor. One or two of them skated just along the edge of punk—well, modified punk, real conservative punk. Still, these young people clearly had eyes and ears for what was happening in the rest of the world, and they were curious, eager to try on some new ideas. Perhaps their curiosity extended to the spiritual. I reflected that, maybe, the most rebellious thing you could possibly do in the Soviet Union was to become a Baptist.

I recognized some of the hymns that the organist played as prelude to the service. "The Church's One Foundation." "A Mighty Fortress Is Our God." Remarkably, the old southern favorite, "Blessed Assurance." My grandmother loved that song, used to sing it in a high, wavering, old-lady soprano voice that spilled out into the house like sunlight pouring through clean windows.

What in the world would Miss Pet make of this, I wondered?

What would she think of the Moscow Baptist Church and me compressed between two babushkas, singing, "Blessed assurance, Jesus is mine! / Oh, what a foretaste of glory divine! / Heir of salvation, purchase of God, / Born of His Spirit, wash'd in His blood . . ."

Well, maybe she saw.

Maybe Miss Pet and Saint Sergius were together on that Holy Thursday, side-by-side, at the communion of saints that reached from the Kingdom of God to the Baptist church at 3 Maly Vuzovsky Per.

The room was plain. There were no candles, no icons. A stained-glass window depicted a cross and a Bible. A banner citing a verse from Corinthians hung over an imposing, carved pulpit. A table below the pulpit was set for the Lord's Supper, recalling that it was on the night before his crucifixion—on Holy Thursday—that Jesus instituted the Eucharist.

After the singing, after lengthy Bible readings and two—count 'em, two—sermons, elders of the congregation distributed bread and wine.

Big loaves of bread—only three or four loaves to serve a thousand—were torn into small pieces and the deep plum-colored wine was poured into twelve large, handsomely chased and etched silver chalices.

The bread and the wine were brought down the aisle to the end of each pew and passed, then, from one of us to the next.

I thought of a night in the First Baptist Church in Bradenton, a long, long time ago, the first time that I had Communion. It was dark outside, and the light within the sanctuary created its own space in a dark world, a little kingdom of light where we were part of a special people, a holy nation, a royal priesthood. Elders passed broken soda crackers among us, and glass thimbles of grape juice.

I didn't know what to do. I grew weary of trying to follow the preacher's retelling of the story of the Last Supper. My mother signaled me when it was time to swallow the piece of soda cracker and the thimble of grape juice: *This do in remembrance of me.*

"This is the body of Christ," I said to the woman beside me.

She answered in Russian.

After the service a woman walking away from the church

with me, showing me the way to the bus stop, waved her hand at all the people moving, in groups of two or three, toward the public transportation stops a few blocks away.

It was quiet and very dark on the steep, narrow street, and the people spoke very quietly to one another.

"All Baptists," the woman told me. "All you see on this street. Baptists."

The Baptists reached a small square and were swallowed by the Soviet world.

12

Time and distance.

The distance becomes blurred, fades, disappears on a train ride on the Arctic Express, thirty-six hours, Moscow to Murmansk. From the air, the rail must look like a pencil line traced a thousand miles down the Central European Plain.

It's the kind of landscape that Dr. Zhivago saw through the slats of the boxcar in the long train sequence from the 1965 film. Cold wilderness. Birch trees and snow. Frozen lakes and rivers. We see animal tracks, imagine wolves, minks, foxes.

Occasionally, unpaved roads, axle-deep in mud, run, briefly, parallel to the railroad track and then turn into the trees. Few cars, a lot of trucks plow through the muck— dump trucks, tractor-trailors hauling timber, tanker trucks.

Country villages are quaint, rough, poor—wooden houses, with little fences and tall trees that are etched against the sky, winter-bare. Privies, tin roofs, television antennae, wash frozen on the clotheslines. A couple of kids romp around on a little hillside with a sled and their dog. We see smoke rising from chimneys and imagine people gathered at kitchen tables. Home.

They call the train an express, but it's a milk run. It stops at every little town, and it stops where there aren't any towns.

All night long, on the first night, we wake up when the train stops and look out the window at some remote, dimly lighted station somewhere in the heart of Russia. People bundled against the cold night in boots, long coats, fur hats cast grotesque, foreshortened shadows. Perhaps they call to one another, but, separated from them by the double glass of the train compartment window, we hear nothing. The silent figures, hurrying across the platform, may be on the most ordinary errands. They look mysterious, alien.

There are nine of us from Jacksonville on the sleeper car in the Arctic Express, en route to Murmansk for an official visit. Murmansk is matched with Jacksonville in the Sister Cities program that promotes person-to-person diplomacy as a means to international understanding.

City council members and representatives of the Sister Cities program, of the mayor's office, and of the Florida Community College of Jacksonville made up the official delegation.

We are met in Moscow by two escorts from Murmansk charged with shepherding us through the long train trip. It was they who discovered the problem with my travel arrangements and dumped me at the Hotel National, raised hell with the Intourist women in person and on the phone with God knows who. Someone in the Kremlin, I imagined. Anyway, they took the rest of the delegation away to dinner while someone, somewhere, got me onto the right train. When I crossed back under Marx Prospekt, the Intourist people loaded me into a car and sent me off through the darkest city streets I've ever seen to 1 Komsomolskaya Square, the Leningrad Railway Station.

The driver handed me over to a dour travel agent in a tiny, private waiting room with a ticket counter, a couple of chairs, and a thick, glass window that looked out on the dim, packed passenger terminal. A dark, muffled flood of people moved past the glass, but I had no sense that they could see me standing there, looking out at them. I wondered if the window were one-way glass. I wondered when I would be reunited with my friends. I thought the train was due to leave Moscow at midnight, and it was almost midnight.

Finally, a young man appeared, grabbed my bag and signaled me to follow him.

I beat the gang to the train.

By a minute or two.

We were glad to see one another.

I hadn't had any supper—truth to tell, I couldn't figure out how to go about getting any food in the hotel. One of my comrades gave me a chocolate bar and another gave me a package of crackers and a little round of Swiss cheese left from our breakfast buffet in Zurich.

We bunked two to a compartment—elsewhere on the train, passengers rode four to a compartment. Our service, called soft seat, is a first-class service. There is a second-class service called hard seat, in which bunks are harder and may number four or six in a compartment.

The narrow bunks aren't bad. The plumbing is. The tea—brewed from an industrial-strength samovar perpetually gurgling at one end of the car—is great. Food, served by appointment in a dining car two cars up-train, is OK. It's our first taste of Russia. Beet and cabbage soup with unfamiliar joints of meat or fowl. Sliced cucumbers and tomatoes. Onion. Salmon caviar. Salami and ham. Beef stroganoff. Bread and butter and cheese. Mineral water.

God-awful mineral water. It tastes like Alka-Seltzer, only not as good, and that's all there is for drinking, even for brushing teeth.

There seems no end to the road from Moscow to Murmansk as the Arctic Express rolls through a night and a day and into the second night.

Lyudmila Eeyevleva comes visiting the second night. She is a pretty woman, red hair, high cheekbones, dark eyes. She wears a neat uniform, and she tells us that she is the "technical lieutenant in charge of the train." That seems to mean that the mechanical operation of the train is the territory of the engineers, but she supervises the care and comfort and feeding of the passengers by the dining-car workers and the samovar women who preside over each car and the hawkers who go through the cars selling candy and sausages and so on.

She tells us that she joined the train service at eighteen because she wanted to travel. "That was fifteen years ago, so you can determine my age," she says, smiling, teasing.

She tells us that she lives in Moscow. She has an eight-year-old son, Jan, who will begin, in a year, to study at the Bolshoi Ballet. She tells us that the train will cross the Arctic Circle sometime around midnight and she asks us if it is true that Michael Jackson is in love with Elizabeth Taylor. She has read this and finds it difficult to believe.

Just friends, we say. Just good friends. She nods seriously.

Jackson is popular in the USSR and so are Billy Joel and Elton John, and Madonna, and the Beatles, and Elvis Presley.

Country music is popular, too. "It is something everyone can understand. The story that happens in the song is the story that happens in everyone's life. The sad story," one of our translators tells us solemnly.

Talk drifts from rock-'n'-roll and country music to English and American literature. In the Soviet Union, the works of Charles Dickens and William Shakespeare, Theodore Dreiser, Mark Twain, Ray Bradbury, and Tennessee Williams are admired.

We do not know when we cross the Arctic Circle—we don't even feel a bump—but we realize that we have talked for a long time and it is past midnight.

The night is clear, the moon almost full. The forest is full of snow. The arctic rolls endlessly by our windows. Cold. Empty.

We are a long way from home. Like Huck and Jim drifting down the Mississippi River on their runaway raft, we are heading into strange territory. And, like Blanche DuBois from Williams's *A Streetcar Named Desire,* we will be depending on the kindness of strangers.

We found nothing else.

Granted, we were official and everybody was supposed to be nice to us. But official and unofficial people seemed genuinely to believe that we were swell.

In a song on the *American Pie* album Don MacLean

sings: "Everybody loves me baby, what's the matter with you, kid."

That was us in Murmansk. Everybody loved us, baby.

Linking Jacksonville and Murmansk as sister cities seems unlikely. Beyond the happenstance that both are ports, there doesn't seem to be much family resemblance.

Murmansk is above the Arctic Circle. The Gulf Stream ensures that the harbor on Kola Bay remains open all year, but the climate is harsh and punishing. The region experiences polar night in the winter, a period of several months when the sun never rises. People work in numbing cold under harsh floodlight and find their way home in the dark. The only sun in Murmansk comes from the sunlamps at the Pioneer Palace, where the children are bathed in artificial summer, sunning under lamps, swimming in a wide, steaming pool.

In summer, Murmansk experiences white nights, when the sun never sets. But even in summertime—average July temperature: about forty-five degrees F—living is not easy in Murmansk. The trees that line the streets are there because somebody planted them and keeps them alive against all odds. There are hardly any trees at all on the rocky hills that fold down to the harbor. Rather, apartment houses grow on the hills, springing up like fairy rings of mushrooms after a rain. They are bleak, cookie-cutter buildings, square and graceless, prefabs, about ten stories. We are told that every year five thousand families move into new flats in Murmansk.

"That was built while I was away. It was not there three months ago," Mayor Vladimir Goryachkin tells us through an interpreter. He waves his hand toward a raw new building, part of a stand of housing being constructed on a hill overlooking the harbor. He sits beside the driver of a van that slips and claws its way up the hill on a steep, muddy, unpaved road intended for heavy equipment.

Goryachkin was fifty years old in 1988. He said he was a boxer, and he looked it: fit and tough and smart. When we arrived he was just back from several months in Moscow, trying to figure out, with other leaders, how to implement perestroika. The Berlin Wall was still up, what was to come would have been unimaginable to any of us, but already there was an uneasy feeling that the old order was on the threshold of profound change.

"This is a revolutionary period, a very important period of our life," Goryachkin told us solemnly. "Its success depends not just on the part of the leaders, but on the part of everyone."

I was there because of the changes, drawn there by them, allowed to be there because of them.

Perestroika. Glasnost. My assignment was to write a series of articles about how perestroika and glasnost looked to an outsider, how it felt for a handful of Russians and for us, their American visitors, in a place that was not a center of power but simply a place where people worked for a living, fishing and handling cargo and buying and selling among themselves and playing and teaching and learning trades and following professions. The delegation of Jacksonville officials gave the story a strong local angle—always a selling point in the newspaper business.

Obviously, I could not write in depth of the historical perspective, the politics or the economics of perestroika and glasnost. We had wire services for that. But I could take this global story and write about what one person saw, heard, felt in the Soviet Union. I could provide the perspective, the point of view, the voice of an observer whom *Times-Union* readers recognized and trusted. My assignment was to do in the Soviet Union what I do in Jacksonville—hold up a mirror and say what we see when we look at ourselves.

So I was a foreign correspondent at last.

And the Soviets were beginning to suspect that perestroika was more than a slogan. Clearly, it was a new and often uncomfortable idea. But hospitality is an old idea in Russia, an idea that is well understood. Our hosts did everything possible to make our visit memorable, from showing off Murmansk's huge fisheries operation to providing a ride on a sleigh pulled by a team of reindeer. The sleigh ride happened at the North Festival Winter Games. The games were begun over a half-century ago and are quite important in northern and eastern Europe. Teams from Sweden, Finland, East Germany, the USA, and various Soviet republics take part in bobsledding, cross-country skiing, skating, reindeer races, and other traditional winter sports. There are also some goofy, nontraditional motorsports on ice—a handful of dinged-up little hot rods, motorcycles and go-carts careening around a frozen race course, having a lot of trouble with traction and going very wide on the turns.

Even goofier was ice-bathing. In North America, the people who do it are called polar bears. The Russians call them walruses. In any language people who chop a hole in the ice and then jump in the water are considered weird.

All of us from Jacksonville left home scared of the cold. We'd seen enough *National Geographic* specials to know what living above the Arctic Circle means. Cold. Cold beyond the power of the human tongue to tell. Ice hanging off our eyebrows, dropping dead in a matter of seconds if we didn't keep moving. Actually, we find, it isn't all that cold. Spring, Murmansk style, is on the way. It's below freezing, but above zero. There's a lot of snow making a lovely crunch under our brand-new boots, but it's beginning to melt. The people in charge of us always are concerned about keeping us warm. They brush us off and bundle us up and scold us about hats and scarves and gloves as if we were children. It's nice to be fussed over.

The kids we meet at the Murmansk Teachers College remind me of kids in the fifties: their hair, their clothes, their manners, their makeup. They are modest, respectful, sweet, innocent. There is something of the same spirit among many adults.

A fashion show is part of the entertainment arranged for us at a meeting with the Soviet-American Friendship Society. The clothes have a stalwart, no-nonsense fifties look. There is nothing decadent or frivolous about these fashions.

In the West much of our popular design grows out of our love affair with aviation and space technology. The Soviet

Union, of course, operates in both of those arenas, but they have not adapted the high-tech look to consumer design.

That's because marketing does not exist in a society of shortages, and without marketing there is no impetus to change design. Marketing calls forth design, pulls new design into being in order to create a demand for it. That hasn't happened in the Soviet Union and so Soviet stuff looks like stuff used to look, in the fifties, the forties, even the thirties. Hotel rooms often look like staterooms on an ocean liner—compact, built-in. TV sets are huge—they must have tubes, not transistors. And phones. They're wonderful. They are square and serious and of another time and place.

Little lace curtains sometimes hang in train windows, and there are lace antimacassars pinned along the top of the seats, shiny wood paneling, table linens—though none too clean—in the dining cars, sullen servers, crafty fox-eyed boys looking for deals, all so much set dressing for an Agatha Christie movie.

Except it is not a set. There is no movie. This is the Soviet Union.

There is a sea adventure tourist attraction in Florida that features a moving sidewalk that slides through a plastic tube at the bottom of a huge tank of sharks. The people move through the sharks and little fishes, among them but oh so separate.

There were times when I felt that I was moving among the Russians like a tourist through the plastic tube at the bottom of the shark tank. I could see them and they could see me, but we inhabited different worlds. I could see what it looked like in the Soviet Union. They knew what it was really like on the other side of the invisible wall.

I think this peculiar isolation was the inevitable consequence of our status as official visitors and of our essential helplessness. We didn't know the language, the customs, the routine, the ropes. We needed leading around by the hand, and our hosts had lined up a small squad of nursemaids for us. They kept us on the move, even paying official calls at the city's huge garbage-burn facility and at the cemetery where graves of foreign merchant marines who died at the Arctic end of the Murmansk run are carefully tended and marked with their flags of national origin.

A boy about fourteen approached me after our visit at the Pioneer Palace with the children who were studying English and were part of the International Club. He said shyly that, during the Great Patriotic War, his grandfather lived for more than a year in Jacksonville, helping to outfit ships for the dangerous Murmansk run that sent supply convoys— often liberty ships, built in Jacksonville—through packs of German submarines, across the North Atlantic, lifelines to Murmansk and Archangel.

"We have letters from him. He stayed at the Floridan Hotel," the boy tells me. A few years ago I watched that hotel implode into a column of dust, and now in Murmansk this Russian boy pulls it back into shape for a moment in his imagination and my memory as he tells me of his grandfather.

I ask if the grandfather still lives in Murmansk.

No, the boy says, he is retired now and lives in the south. However, he adds solemnly, he will write to him and tell him that he has met with people from Jacksonville and brought greetings.

I thank him.

It is a sweet encounter.

There is little time in Murmansk for sweet encounters or to reflect on all that we see and hear and wonder about. Our hosts roust us out early and keep us on the run into the night. I stay awake at night simply to claim some time for myself to absorb what we've seen. I sit at the desk in my room in the Arctika Hotel and look out on a city square with a geometric design shoveled clear of snow, the snow cleared out of the design piled high alongside the walkways. Every night, along about midnight, I see a little white dog materialize, trot around the square until she finds the right spot for her mission, and then disappear back into the darkness. She's a cheerful spirit down there in the middle of Murmansk with the square all to herself.

Every night I look out on the square for an hour or so. I see two or three cars in an hour, perhaps one streetcar, sometimes a person, bundled in the cold, going somewhere, home, I suppose, and, always, the little white dog.

After a week in Murmansk the Jacksonville delegation heads home—and I head south, to Leningrad and Moscow. Nine days alone in the Soviet Union sounds like it could get hairy. When the driver delivers me to the airport for the Murmansk-Leningrad flight, for the first time it's up to me to figure out the system, and it's a little scary and a lot baffling.

In international politics we always are trying to figure out whether to trust the Russians. I have no choice. I have to trust them. I get on the plane for Leningrad.

Aeroflot.

We've never heard anything good about Aeroflot, right? We vaguely imagine that passengers are issued army blankets and a heel of black bread at the door. Nope. It's a little cramped, but it's OK. It's adequate.

I think of my arrival in Moscow more than a week ago now, of looking out at the Aeroflot planes on the runways at Sheremetyevo, the red hammer-and-sickle emblem stenciled on their tails, the Cyrillic letters that identified them, the unsmiling young guards in their fur hats and long coats and high boots looking something like the flying monkeys from *The Wizard of Oz*.

It looked so alien then.

It looks so different now.

It is no longer all processed through imagination and expectation.

There is a real country out there now.

I am off to see a little piece of it.

13

There may be a million ghosts in Leningrad. Or there may be no such thing as ghosts, and it is simply history that haunts Leningrad.

"It is still difficult to say how many people died in the siege. There are estimates from 650,000 to 1.2 million. You see, some people who were alive at the end of the siege died after, of the effects," an Intourist guide, Dimitri, tells me. "Truckloads of dead were brought to mass graves. Some days, three to four thousand in a single day. Some days, ten to twelve thousand. Truckloads of dead."

The siege began in September 1941 and continued until January 1943. The population of Leningrad in 1941 was approximately three million. Some of the dead were killed in bombardment. Most of the dead starved.

It is an image made more awful by the uncanny beauty of the city.

Leningrad is built along a river, a bit reminiscent of London or Paris. It is a city meant for walking, built in proportions that are not overwhelming. Again, like London and the heart of Paris, the city is manageable, one might almost say "user-friendly." There are no skyscrapers, but rather the handsome and dignified neoclassical architecture of the eighteenth and nineteenth centuries.

It is a city of wide boulevards, of great courtyards and

public squares, of the Winter Palace and the Hermitage, of the Kirov Theater, of St. Isaac's Cathedral. But the city has more than buildings and bridges. It has always had a rich life of the mind and spirit. It nurtured modern Russian literature—Pushkin, Gogol, Dostoevsky are closely associated with Leningrad. Tchaikovsky and Rachmaninoff are buried here. Pavlova, Nijinsky, and Ulanova set out from Leningrad on tours that revolutionized dance for the world.

It is the Venice of the North, the city built as Peter the Great's window on Europe. Peter, who ruled Russia from 1682 until 1725, founded the city, on the shores of the Baltic Sea, in 1703. From that time until the Revolution of 1917, the city was capital of the empire. It was known as St. Petersburg. After the Revolution the city was renamed Petrograd and, finally, after Lenin's death, in 1924, renamed again in his honor.

But a city doesn't inhabit its past.

Peter was insatiably curious about the West and determined to pull Russia toward Europe and the sea. He built a museum in his city, called Peter's Chamber of Curiosities. On the plaza in front of Peter's Chamber of Curiosities, kids ride skateboards. Nearby, tourists queue outside the Hermitage, waiting to see what many consider the world's greatest art collection. They stand near the spot where Czar Nicholas II's orders to his soldiers to disperse a demonstration of workers led, in 1905, to a massacre called Bloody Sunday that nurtured the seeds of revolution. Shoppers at a grocery market a few blocks away fill string bags with tomatoes, canned fish, cheese, milk, potatoes, beef, tea.

Kids skateboard. Shoppers shop.

Life goes on. The past recedes.

Or does it?

Just outside the city, at Piskarevskoye Memorial Cemetery, the past is present. More than 500,000 victims of the siege are buried here in mass graves and visitors stream endlessly through the cemetery, coming from Leningrad and from all over the world.

There is an eternal flame, a massive image of Mother Russia, a wall of bas-relief figures depicting the defenders of Leningrad. Dirge-like music plays over a sound system. Row after row of great mounds of earth, landscaped, the corners neatly sculpted, are carefully kept and people wander among them silently.

Carl Sandburg must have seen a place like this in his head when he wrote "Grass"—"Pile the bodies high at Austerlitz and Waterloo. Shovel them under and let me work—."

Shovel them under and let me work.

The Soviet Union tends its past.

This is what the nation has vowed about the Great Patriotic War, 1941–1945, which cost twenty million Russian lives: "Nothing and No One Shall Be Forgotten."

Intourist buses fill and overflow the large parking area outside the cemetery entrance. Outside the gates, kiosks offer for sale histories of the siege, guides to the cemetery. A young woman sells single carnations for a few kopeks, to leave at the eternal flame or at the feet of Mother Russia.

Mother Russia.

Where does the thought of Mother Ginger, the cheerful, rotund character from *The Nutcracker* with children pouring out from under her aprons, come from? She is an image of Mother Russia, too, I suppose, her children tumbling out from her skirts on a stage where dancers give body to Tchaikovsky's music. Other themes from Tchaikovsky pour into the chill air from the loud speakers above our heads, music for Mother Russia who has buried millions at her feet.

Icons, images, metaphor are part of the Russian way of understanding life. Old Russia and socialist Russia are poet nations, mystic nations. Nothing is exactly as it seems. It is more. Always more.

Mother Russia watches over her dead children.

And once the czar was seen as a father figure. And more. A painting of Christ depicted as a czar is pointed out by a guide in the Cathedral of St. Peter and St. Paul, where Peter the

Great and most of his successors are buried. "The idea was that Christ was czar of heaven, as the czar was ruler of Earth," she says.

Now there's an idea to push some buttons. I bristle, think that it's no wonder they had a revolution, they must have needed one. I study the imperious Christ looking back at me from the painting on the cathedral wall.

I could never pray in Russia.

It was the oddest thing. I've always said my prayers before I go to sleep at night. I suppose it may be my oldest voluntary, cognitive behavior. Now I lay me down to sleep—or words to that effect, every night, from age three or so. How many prayers? About twenty thousand I guess. That must have cut some kind of pattern, some mini-Natchez Trace in my brain. But, in Russia, I couldn't find it, not very often.

I looked at the czar/Christ in the cathedral/museum in Leningrad, and I thought that the two of us didn't have anything to say to each other. We had never met before. He was the one the old women in the cathedrals at Zagorsk worshipped. I was a long way from home.

The Peter and Paul Fortress is a graceless chunk of masonry on tiny Zayachi Ostrove (Hare Island), across the Neva River from the Hermitage. It was built by Peter the Great as a refuge where he could live while supervising the construction of his new capital. In the early eighteenth century, the fortress became a prison and one of its first prisoners was Peter's son Alexis, who was tortured to death in the dungeon for conspiring against his father.

Catherine the Great also had use for the prison—she had Princess Tarakanova dispatched there, and she imprisoned one of Russia's first revolutionaries, the aristocrat Alexander Radischev, there. Leon Trotsky and Maxim Gorky were jailed in the fortress after the 1905 revolution.

On the day that I was there, the walruses (those human polar bears) were lined up along the walls of the fortress. They were stripped, some to their underwear, and they leaned against the thick walls that stored heat from the sun, even when there's not much heat to store. Every now and then, one of them jumped into the Neva and paddled around among the chunks of ice.

Don't ask.

No one knows.

Just down the river from the Peter-and-Paul Fortress, the old cruiser *Aurora* is moored. Another of those shots heard 'round the world was fired from her fo'c's'le gun on October 25, 1917. It marked the beginning of the October Revolution that changed Russia forever and then changed the world forever. The ship is an historic exhibit, but it is also a commissioned ship in the Soviet navy. At sundown the bugle is blown and the flag comes down. In the morning it is raised again.

My hotel—the Leningrad on Pirogovskaya Embankment—is directly across the river from the *Aurora*. I snap the photograph from my window that becomes the signature of the series of articles for the *Florida Times-Union.*

In the photograph the Neva is polished pewter, still as a lake, almost free of ice, and the *Aurora* and the pastel buildings behind it are reflected perfectly, as if in a mirror. It's a stunning, evocative photograph. We call the series "Russia: Images of the Soviet Union."

At night I turn out the light in my room and sit in the dark, looking across the river at the shape of the old ship, black against a few city lights in the buildings beyond it.

I have the shark tank feeling again.

In the morning, a formation of cadets from the Nakhimov Naval Academy wakes me up, calling cadence as they jog past the *Aurora*. The Neva is full of ice again, but it is a spring day, full of promise.

At breakfast, I meet a group of visitors from Cuba. I tell them that I am from Florida. It's like running into somebody from the old neighborhood. We share a table and try our best to have a conversation.

I want to spend the day wandering in Leningrad, no agenda, no particular expectations.

It's sunny, almost warm. A convoy of military trucks rumbles along the Embankment. Otherwise, there's not much other traffic. A couple of kids balancing skateboards on their heads amble past. An old woman carrying a string bag holding a bunch of spring onions and a square of cheese pauses on Pirogovskays Boulevard and looks across the icy Neva at the *Aurora*.

It is little tableau of Leningrad, or a tapestry, a tapestry woven of past and present and future.

I walk down to the corner and hop a trolley, a clanking, old-fashioned trolley—the kind that Judy Garland rode in *Meet Me in St. Louis*—and ride it full circle. That's a good way to see any city. The car snakes back away from the wide boulevards, and it's like exploring the cupboards and back halls of a great palace.

We pass two women—coworkers in municipal service, apparently—who wear khaki work aprons and whose tools include a large spoon and a hammer and whose assignment is apparently to dig muck out of the grates that cover manholes. Two young soldiers lounge near a kiosk, eating ice cream cones, watching the world go by. A woman positions her toddler behind a wall to shield him from the view of passersby on the sidewalk, and rearranges his clothing so that he can urinate. Outside a hospital four people in white coats gather in a companionable circle near an ambulance entrance, smoking cigarettes. It seems that everyone in the Soviet Union—all the men, anyway—smoke cigarettes. They smoke in the European style, holding the cigarette between the thumb and the first two fingers.

The trolley is almost empty, and we rumble back through a poor area where the streets are narrow and unpaved and the buildings look grim. Leningrad still has some old communal housing—apartments where several families share sanitary and kitchen facilities. I am told that replacing them with private apartments for everyone is a high priority in the Soviet Union. I hope so. But I do not believe that it has happened. Urban renewal, Leningrad-style, means that the elegant facades of the eighteenth-century buildings are preserved while the insides are pulled out like gutting a fish. The trolley passes a lot of these gutted fishes.

A cat—the first I've seen in Russia—suns his tawny hide in a doorway. An old woman, bent, bundled in a dark coat, dark stockings, a long dark scarf, a dark knit cap, steps cautiously over him and moves slowly down the sidewalk. I subtract forty-five years from her age and wonder if she added a son or a little daughter, a mother, a husband to the trucks that prowled through Leningrad's ruined streets during the siege, collecting thousands of bodies each day for burial at Piskarevskoye Cemetery. She carries a string bag with her.

All the babushkas—the grandmothers—carry string bags when they go out. One of their jobs is to keep an eye out for scarce items, and then they stand in line to buy a handful of onions, potatoes, tomatoes, beets, cucumbers. Standing in line is part of the day in the life of just about everybody in the USSR. Shortages are real and unpredictable. Set up a table on the sidewalk and arrange a display of anything—shoestrings, buttons, scarves, radishes—and everyone who passes will at least pause to see whether it's an item the household needs.

The grandmothers, because they are often pensioners and have the time, are always shopping. The grandmothers have other jobs, too. They are often attendants at museums and historic attractions. They keep up the churches. They clean the streets, and that's a surprising sight, at first, and I think it doesn't seem respectful to have ice chipped away and streets swept by old women. But they don't seem unhappy about it. I ask a woman chipping ice off the hotel steps if I may take her photograph and she's proud to pose and gives me a grin that glitters with the metal dental restorations favored in Eastern Europe and she's obviously got heart and soul and a cheerful spirit along with stainless-steel teeth and a job shoveling snow off the sidewalk.

Old women aren't delicate, at least not in Russia. They have survived more than most of us can imagine, and there's

victory in survival, even if it costs eternal sorrow to remember what was lost. Russia's old women have authority.
They can speak to any child with the expectation that the
child will obey, and the child's parents will not object. They
are guardians, keepers of continuity with the past.

Young couples in the USSR traditionally come straight
from their wedding ceremony to place flowers at a war memorial, thus recognizing the sacrifices of their parents and
grandparents in the Great Patriotic War and pledging themselves to continue to defend, and build, the state. In a sense,
I reflect, the authority granted to the babushkas is a sort of
tribute to what has gone before. It is the children and the
grandchildren of the old women laying flowers at their feet.

They are Mother Russia.

They sit in parks and watch the children play.

They stand in line with string bags, waiting to buy spring
onions.

They have buried millions.

14

Moscow street scene.

A few blocks from Red Square, near the Karl Marx Prospekt metro station, a couple of women have set up shop. They have piled baskets and baskets of produce along a stone wall and are selling tomatoes, cucumbers, basil, and spring onions. They have scales to weigh the goods, an abacus to count what is owed them, and more customers than they can count. Everyone is quiet, very serious about their transactions with the tomato sellers.

Next to the impromptu vegetable stand, two young men are peddling vegetable peelers, the kind advertised on cable TV around Christmas time, the ones that turn beets and potatoes into works of decorative art with a twist of the wrist. The salesmen have a good show going—one talking, one twisting out veggie art. Everyone watches and listens carefully.

Everyone is very, very solemn.

The men deliver their sales pitch as seriously as the guides in the Lenin Museum, a few blocks away, deliver their learned lectures. The folk listen as intently as the eager little Pioneers and the earnest college students and the foreign tourists listen to the museum lectures.

It all looks pretty grim for something as frivolous as the buying and selling of a kitchen gadget. But it doesn't feel grim; it feels good. Comfortable and safe and quiet. Kind of down-home, really, given that Moscow's population is nine million and that some of the nine million are among the most powerful people on earth and that strings are pulled in Moscow that tug events around the world.

Maybe it's the generations of socialism, the collective mentality, the basic character of the people, some combination of all of the above, but Moscow is a laid-back kind of place, a plain, primitive Southern California in winter white and institutional gray. All over the world, big city means competition for space and grace, life in the fast lane. But Moscow keeps its own pace.

I'm comfortable wandering off the beaten path, within reason, of course, and exploring the beaten paths independently. Official guides have all the facts and love to share them. But learning the weight and dimensions of the red stars on top of the Kremlin watchtowers—a ton each, six feet from tip to tip—can't hold a candle to just hanging out on Red Square, people watching.

There are people there from all over the world, mostly taking one another's pictures in front of Lenin's tomb and waiting for the changing of the guards. That happens every hour. Three soldiers—inevitably young, good-looking, solemn—goose step out of Savior Gate Tower and proceed 150 yards or so to the mausoleum where the earthly remains of Vladimir Ilyich Lenin (1870–1924) are preserved and, in fact, displayed five days a week.

It's not news that he's there, of course, but just how deeply odd it seems to the Westerner to display the embalmed remains of a national hero really sinks in.

We wouldn't do that even with Elvis Presley.

Would we?

Well . . .

Another spot for posing for those proof-that-I-was-there pictures is in front of St. Basil's Cathedral, also known as the Cathedral of St. Basil the Blessed, the Cathedral of the Intercession, or Pokrovsky Cathedral. It is Russia's signature cathedral, the one with lots of colors and nine onion domes. It was built in the sixteenth century on the orders of Ivan the Terrible. He was so pleased with it that he had his architects' eyes put out so that they never could build another like it. That's one of the reasons they called him terrible.

Opposite the Kremlin, there's G.U.M., the Soviet Union's largest and most famous—well, only famous—department store. It might be better understood as the granddaddy of the Western world's multilevel mall, rather than as a single department store. It is arranged on three levels in a nine-teenth-century building. There are several hundred shops—many closer to stalls than to actual shops—where every-thing from groceries to lace hankies and luggage and shower curtains is for sale. The store is crowded.

If Napoleon sneered that the English were a nation of shopkeepers, he might have described the Russians as a nation of shoppers. Not that anyone cares much what Napo-leon said—a winter in Moscow and a summer in Waterloo shattered his credibility.

It's almost time to go home. So it's time to join the shop-pers. Getting around Moscow by bus and metro is not diffi-cult, especially with a note written in Russian, by someone from Intourist, that says where the bearer of the note wants to go. Studying it helps you recognize street and station names, if you're determined to do it all by yourself. If you give up, the note makes it easy to ask for help.

Paddington Bear, standing in the railroad station with a label pinned to his coat that says "Take care of this bear," is the feeling.

I buy fur hats for me and the kids, Russian cigarettes and chocolate, some handsome wooden things—boxes and carv-ings and spoons and so on—to pass around back home.

I set out one morning to find a bookstore to buy some Russian children's books, and a Russian language edition of *Gone with the Wind* for a friend. I don't know how I ever find the place—I begin the quest on the underground, eventually move above ground and take a couple of buses, walk blocks, study the Cyrillic letters that mark the streets, comparing them with the address written for me by the Intourist woman at the hotel.

I feel guided now by radar, or angels, rather than the address on the paper. I have lost track of myself.

Well, Ms. Intourist had told me it was complicated to find the place, that I ought to take a taxi.

I told her, no, I could find it.

I did.

And I found Scarlett O'Hara, sitting in the cool shade of the porch at Tara, overlooking the savagely red land, blood-colored after rains, brick dust in droughts, the best cotton land in the world.

It was good to see a familiar face, or at least to know that the familiar face was in there somewhere, hidden in the Cyrillic alphabet.

I turned through the pages and wished I could read it.

I needed to touch some familiar territory.

I was finally getting homesick, and homesick alone in Moscow is homesick indeed.

On my final Sunday in the Soviet Union, I filed a story from the AP bureau. Oh, I didn't ever want to leave that little haven. It was a capsule of home. There were a couple of word processors, a newswire with dispatches clattering in from other Russian cities. There were clocks that told the time in London and New York. There were English-language news-papers and magazines and books scattered all over the place, and there was a nice guy running the bureau and we talked shop for a little while before I headed back to my hotel.

I hopped a bus. I didn't know where it was going, but I figured that, eventually, I'd recognize something, and I did.

The Kremlin.

In Alexandrovsky Garden I watched a newly married cou-ple leave her bouquet at the Tomb of the Unknown Soldier. She wore a long white wedding dress and a band of flowers in her smooth dark hair, and he wore a well-cut three-piece blue suit and he was broad-shouldered, athletic, blond. They placed an armful of long-stemmed orange and red and pink flowers on the paving stones before the eternal flame that was pulled into a restless little dance by an early spring wind that moved erratically through the garden and across the square.

I watched the couple and their families pose for pictures, arranging and rearranging themselves in various combinations. After a few minutes I left them to their documenting and walked around the corner to Red Square. A few weeks ago it had been a movie set, a scene from my imagination, a mysterious island floating under a dark sky marked by the constellation of the cross, the moon, the red star. The people themselves had seemed to form a faceless subterranean river flowing in more mystery through the pedestrian crosswalk underneath Marx Prospekt. Russians . . .

They were no longer faceless.

I had not solved the mystery, untangled the metaphor, but I thought of the words that Jody Baxter speaks to Ma in the opening of *The Yearling*, Marjorie Kinnan Rawlings's novel of pioneer Florida: "I seen me a sight today, Ma."

Well, I had seen me some sights in the Soviet Union—and some people.

I still think of them every day.

I think of the pious old women who live less in this world than the next, and I think of the young couple leaving flowers at the Tomb of the Unknown Soldier on their wedding day.

And I think of me, on Red Square, that first night.

Here's looking at you, kid.

Ain't That America

15

Just north of Dover, Arkansas, I cross a creek and see people standing on the bank, in the shadow of the narrow old bridge. There's a man out in the creek, about thigh-deep—a preacher, I realize—and a few people are standing in the creek around him, waiting to be baptized.

I pull off the road, walk down to the creek bank, stand just at the edge of a dozen or so who are gathered there. The preacher talks about the example set by Jesus at the River Jordan, and then he baptizes a young woman and a boy about twelve and a man and his wife who wear blue jeans and red T-shirts that match.

They wade out of the creek, their clothes and hair plastered flat, water streaming down their faces, looking touched by glory and self-conscious and happy.

They get hugged as they reach the edge of the creek, hugged and patted and cried over and the preacher says, "Sing! Ever'body sing!"

> *Shall we gather at the river,*
> *the beautiful, the beautiful river,*
> *Gather with the saints at the river*
> *that flows by the throne of God . . .*

I introduce myself and say that it has been a long, long

time since I've seen a baptism like this, and I hope they don't mind that I stopped.

They say that I am welcome, as welcome as I can be, that they are glad that I turned off the road and came down to the creek.

There's not many people getting saved anymore, the preacher says. Only a few. He asks me: Is it the same in Florida?

I tell him I don't know. I don't know how many are getting saved in Florida, but I expect it's about the same everywhere, and that not nearly as many as need to be saved have heard the good news.

I've lost track of all the country roads I didn't turn down because I was on a schedule, in an interstate hurry to get from one spot to another. Now there's a catchy chorus for a truck–drivin' country song—"I'm in an interstate hurry, honey, to get back home to you . . ."

A year or so after I came home from the Soviet Union, I caught up on some of those country roads.

I wanted to see America. I wanted to spend some time with myself. I knew a few people along the way—mainly cousin Phyllis at Mount St. Scholastica—but mostly I was among strangers, and, as the preacher in Arkansas said, I was welcome, as welcome as I could be.

I met some women cleaning tubs of big, ugly gar fish under a shed on the poor side of Lake Providence, Louisiana. It takes sweat and muscle and big ragged-edged knives and pliers to peel the hide off these monsters. Blood splatters everywhere—flies buzz, the half-grown cat that hangs out under the shed licks her chops—and it's a mess, but the women are laughing and kidding and helping each other out. Could I watch for a while? I ask.

You're welcome, they say.

I ask how they cook gar fish.

Shake a little flour on 'em, or breading, they tell me. Or just salt and pepper 'em and use some garlic powder. Fry 'em. They're good, not too strong, taste something like crawfish.

They say I should stay for dinner.

My Uncle Whit and some of his friends had a fish camp way east in Manatee County out on the Braden River. There was nothing much there but a shed with a big screened porch and an outhouse. Scrub country. Snakes and mosquitoes and wild pigs galore. Slash pine. Some blackjack oak. Palmetto. Deep sand, white as a gulf beach right along the bank of the twisty little river. The river was the color of strong brewed tea. Besides the bream and the bass the men went up there to catch and cook to eat with their raw whiskey and hushpuppies and grits and heart o' palm, there were alligator turtles in the river that could take your finger off with a single snap and there were gar fish.

Nobody wanted to catch them.

They were trash fish, everybody said.

Couldn't get the skin off 'em. It was like leather. They tasted like mud. Nobody would eat 'em, somebody said.

Well, only colored people, somebody observed, and everybody nodded. That was the truth.

The gars hung still in the water against the current, prehistoric shadows. Their long, sawtooth snouts were evolution's inelegant version of the swords of the lofty marlin. The gars lined up and held steady in formation across the current, like old serfs with antique farm implements at the ready. The gar were big, and I wanted to know if they'd hurt you with their saws—I thought of them as sawfish—and my uncle said no, they wouldn't hurt you, they just weren't any good, that was all.

It kept getting cold and colder all that day at my uncle's fish camp, on the day that I saw the gar fish. It must have been freezing by dark. There was a big campfire, roaring and hissing like it could suck a small animal, maybe even a child, into it. The night was so clear you could see through it millions and millions of miles. The pinewood fire threw pieces of itself at the night like it was fighting back at the stars, a stream of hot little points of light, like tracer bullets. We sat around the fire and our faces were hot, burning hot, and our backs were cold. I watched and shivered and listened. The grownups talked and passed around a bottle of vodka and splashed it into their coffee mugs. Vodka. Everybody talked about the vodka because it was before anybody drank vodka as a regular thing in Florida's piney woods. They were drinking it because the guest of honor that night was a journalist, a foreign correspondent home from Moscow, and he was married to a Russian woman.

A white Russian, that was what I had heard my parents call her on the way out to the country. I was sitting in the backseat of the Chevrolet with the running board, hoping they'd let me ride on the running board a little ways when we got to the clearing by the river, staring out the window, listening to their conversation, to the edge of the conversation. I wondered what that meant, a white Russian. I asked. They told me something, but I didn't understand their answer.

So I sat there in the circle around the fire in the middle of that pitch-dark, freezing Florida night and I stared at the woman married to the foreign correspondent. I think I remember that she was very pretty, orange light from the fire dancing over her long hair and her face that I knew was not like our faces, though I could not have said why. And I wondered what color other Russians were.

The black women of Lake Providence, Louisiana, repeat their invitation. Stay for dinner, they say.

I can't, I tell them. I've got to keep moving.

One of them says she's seen me before. Last night, she says. Didn't she see me at the carnival out on the edge of town? I'm traveling with the carnival, aren't I?

I grin. I kind of nod. Hey, don't I wish. Just for a little while . . .

Driving down a country road, it is easy to believe that there is a *Brigadoon* version of America just around the bend, a place where America is just the way it used to be. But that's illusion. Nothing is the way it used to be. Satellite dishes and Wal-Mart stores tie us all into a single and infinitely complex tapestry that is ever on the loom.

It's almost the year 2000.

Everything has changed.

The places that look like family farms may be owned by agribusiness or the bank, and the bank may be owned by the Japanese. The little churches in the shady groves on America's country roads may look the same as they did the last time the century turned, but their role has changed. They are no longer the only gathering place for miles around, the central repository of wisdom and respectability. They're one alternative in a pluralistic society. It's not easy to be a pluralistic society. We're trying to learn how, but we don't have precedents. So we wish there were a *Brigadoon* America; we wish that things were like they used to be.

It's no wonder.

We're making up the present as we go along. There's no other way to do it, and sometimes it feels like we've pulled ourselves up by the roots or sheared our pin off clean on a submerged log and we're drifting.

Drifting.

We need an anchor, a vision of America where things make sense, like they did once upon a time. We remember an echo of a kind of music, a kind of poetry, in America that we strain to hear again. Oh, the names. The names of our country churches are pure poetry.

The Baptists seem to have a special knack for it. I collect church names for four thousand miles, all the way to Nebraska and home again. Our sacred groves and their little meeting houses have a special sweetness in the South, but that's no surprise.

Harmony Church.

Baptized Believers Church of the Living God, Inc.

Camp Joy Rescue Mission Farm.

Shady Grove Baptist Church.

Happy Valley Baptist Church.

Mount Lovely Baptist Church.

North Star Baptist Church.

The End Time Handmaidens of Jasper, Ark.

And the names of creeks and rivers have their own music, especially when they hold echoes of the Indians who were here from the beginning.

Mississippi.

Mississippi.

Mississippi.

Listen.

Listen to it.

The Father of Waters.

What have we lost?

The Indians understood something about America that we no longer understand. Joseph Campbell, the distinguished mythologist, discussed in his work the belief among primitive people that the land they inhabited and all its inhabitants were sacred, charged with spiritual power. I wonder what America would be if we understood it as charged with spiritual power rather than as so much real estate. I wonder how America would be different if we saw ourselves, now that the buffalo and the panther are gone, as the land's sacred creatures.

Well, maybe we do see it that way. Some of us.

People are shaped by the places that nurture them. I thought of that in Plains, Georgia. It was late afternoon when I pulled over and stopped on the main drag. Everything was closed. That was OK. I didn't want to buy anything. I didn't want to talk to anybody. I wanted to remember.

I was in the House of Representatives that night in September 1978 when President Jimmy Carter announced the Camp David Accord in a speech to the Congress, the Washington diplomatic corps, the Joint Chiefs of Staff. Menachem Begin and Anwar Sadat were there, sitting with Rosalynn Carter, directly across the gallery from where I sat.

It was a remarkable night, a night when ordinary men brought the world to the threshold of a most extraordinary possibility: peace.

That was the feeling in the House—and it was overwhelming. Emotion rolled up from the floor. Emotion rolled down from the galleries—packed standing room only with dignitaries, press, and a few ordinary visitors in the right place at the right time. We did not weep openly, but neither was every eye dry. We knew we were present at a moment when eternal longings touched politics and history and human courage.

The sense of risk-taking for the sake of the oldest and greatest of all prizes—peace on earth—charged that spare and historic room with the kind of energy that could cause stones to cheer if we had not been there to do it. Hope. Risk. Faith. I looked at those men that night—at Carter, Begin, Sadat—and I thought how odd that men who looked so ordinary had brought the world to this moment.

The act that gathered the evening into a single image came seconds after President Carter left the room. Begin and Sadat—men whose nations have been enemies for three decades—faced each other in the gallery. They seemed to look across worlds and ages and innumerable deaths at one another.

Then they embraced.

Nothing in my life has more profoundly affected me, and it has never stopped affecting me, and I don't think it ever will. Someday, I may be pessimistic about the future. I suppose, if life were grim enough, despair would be part of my political vocabulary. But after that night, after the speech, after watching those three men I will never be a cynic.

I wandered around Plains and sorted through it again.

Plains is as ordinary as a place can be. It's the kind of place kids leave before the principal's signature on their high-school diploma is dry. But it feels . . . feels what? Real. Connected. A good man from Plains would risk Camp David, would believe that it could happen and ask his mother to pray for its success.

The light at the end of the day is gold, pure gold.

Most of the time, I bypass interstates.

In Mississippi, or maybe it's Missouri, I point to a thin line traced on my map and ask a man the way to the road.

"That's a pig track, ma'am, and there's two bridges out. You go that way, you'll never get there. You want the interstate."

Sometimes, it's the only way to go.

I tag a van for miles that has ruffled curtains swaying across the rear windows, a three-tone paint job, a spare tire that reads: "The Wilsons, 8 children, 17 grandchildren, 5 great-grandchildren." Two of those yellow cardboard squares with suction cups are stuck on the side window: *Grandma on Board. Grandpa on Board.* There's a bumper sticker that says the Wilsons have been to the Bowling Hall of Fame.

In Tupelo, Mississippi, I spend an hour leaning against a fence, watching men and their little boys play baseball in a schoolyard in the late afternoon, around suppertime.

The next morning, I visit Elvis's birthplace, and then I head north, up Highway 78 to Memphis. Along the stretches of 78 where the highway is still a two-lane country road, there is quiet, rich land and pretty little crossroads towns with big Baptist churches that look solid as the rock of ages. These days the country doesn't feel poor, but if you know anything at all, you know that thirty, forty, fifty years ago just about everybody was poor.

Vernon and Gladys Presley were about as poor as people can be in 1948 when they packed everything they owned into a 1937 Plymouth and headed north, all their options in Tupelo played out, moving one hundred miles to Memphis to look for work.

Today it's impossible to drive along Highway 78 with Elvis on your mind and not see the road as a metaphor for the singer's life and career. The road from Tupelo to Memphis turned out to be the road to incredible fame and fortune for the Presleys.

I think of thirteen-year-old Elvis, a sweet little old country boy, desperately poor, probably scared, looking out the window at the highway taking him away from everything he knew, toward something he could never have dreamed.

Or did he?

Maybe he dreamed it all, saw it before it happened.

In 1971 Presley was named one of seven Outstanding Young Men of the Year by the American Junior Chamber of Commerce. In his acceptance speech, Presley said: "When I was young, I was the hero of the comic books I read. I saw movies, and I was the hero of the movie. So every dream that

I ever dreamed has come true a hundred times."

Rags-to-riches is the classic American dream.

There are two places to see just how poor Elvis was, growing up. You can see it in the two-room house where he was born. And you can see it in Graceland. It's the perfect set for the classic American dream, part II. That's the sequel, the part of the tale when we tell one another that all the money in the world can't make us happy if we're all alone.

Funny, isn't it? That's how we understand Presley's death, though he was not alone. We see him almost as a prisoner in Graceland, surrounded by people who did not love him enough to save him from himself.

A peculiar and oddly touching element of the Elvis phenomenon is how many people entertain the secret notion that, just given a chance, they could have helped Elvis. They think that they could have been the friend, the brother, the mother, the lover that the King needed to save his life.

It's a naive idea.

But it's a fantasy that good people would entertain, not bad people.

Elvis touched us. He was the dark side and the bright side of the American dream. The myth is genuine.

He touched us.

Kansas City pops up on the horizon pretty much like the Emerald City of Oz, by golly.

I slide along the expressway, cool and comfortable, surrounded by wraparound Haydn, confident that Atchison and the Mount St. Scholastica Convent, where my cousin lives, are an hour away.

In the Soviet Union part of reform was to publish correct maps. Before glasnost/perestroika, maps of the USSR were said to be purposely erroneous in order to keep everyone, especially potential invaders, confused. Not in the USA. Our maps work. I love running a fluorescent yellow marker from Jacksonville to Kansas in confidence that there's a reality out on the road that matches the marks on the map.

I find the Leavenworth-Atchison exit. This part of Kansas isn't the textbook idea of Kansas, the monotonous pictures of dusty plains spread out to the horizon, flat and featureless as an ironed sheet. This part of Kansas is pretty and green, rolls gently under farms, orchards, little towns, keeps its feet wet in the Missouri River.

But the sky feels wider out here.

I entertain a fantasy that it's no accident that Amelia Earhart grew up in Atchison. It's the sky—there's so much of it. Maybe she was drawn to explore it the way a kid who grows up by the ocean wants to be a sailor.

I pull into the parking lot at the convent just at suppertime, as promised a week ago when I left Florida, and my cousin is waiting.

I feel like Marco Polo, arrived from a long journey, with a tale to tell.

What was it like, she asks me, driving across America?

I tell her, *It's something to see.*

16

In a neighborhood antique shop I spotted a little stack of flat tin boxes, each about three inches square: Between the Acts Little Cigars. I picked up one of the tins, opened it.

The bit of wax paper that once was folded over the little cigars to keep them fresh was in place, still crisp, its quaint illustration of two gentlemen in top hats and evening wear perfectly clear. Each gentleman held a little cigar with a carefully made plume of smoke balanced above it. The illustration was designed in perfect symmetry.

The little cigars were gone. There was not a speck of tobacco, no trace, not even a faint scent of it in the little tin box.

I asked the shop owner how much she wanted for a cigar tin.

One dollar.

I paid her and took the tin home and put it on my desk, by a photograph of my father.

There is a little cigar tin now on both sides of the glass— one in the twenty-five-year-old photographic image, there on my father's desk; the other on my desk. Image and reality reflect one another. It is a design, imperfect symmetry.

My father, Dewey Albert Dye, has been dead for twenty-two years. But when I saw those cigar tins in the antique store, I could see him lighting up, the hint of theatricality in the measured way he shook out the match and the way he used the cigar to emphasize a point in conversation, to introduce a pause.

Oh my, the man could talk.

He loved words. They were the tools of his trade—journalism for a little while, and then the law. He was informed and funny and lively, listening with the same skill with which he spoke. And both skills arose from his boundless, affectionate curiosity about people and the world.

I think of him every day.

But, every now and then, suddenly, unexpectedly I see him in the oddest corners of my life, in, for instance, the cigar tins stacked on the dusty table in the back of the antique store.

I see him shaking out the match, arching an eyebrow, leaning forward to engage most fully in the conversation.

And I trade a dollar for a little piece of the memory, for a tin box, something tangible of the indelible image.

There are so many ways to remember people.

One is remembering people in things, the things that they touched and used. Those memories are attached to the physical, rooted in the senses rather than in the mind. I think perhaps they are less processed than memories rooted in the mind, that they are a more direct path to the past. I think they are the most evocative of all memories. They are the memories that hold detail.

Wax paper.

When I was a child, my father fixed my lunch for school every morning. I would sit at the kitchen table and we would talk—often of the progress of the war, and we would look at illustrations in the morning paper of maps crisscrossed by thick arrows and tiny tanks and soldier shapes. He would interpret, and I would listen and watch him stir up a concoction of cream cheese and chopped olives, spread it on white bread, trim off the crusts, wrap the sandwich with the most wonderful precision in wax paper. The folds were crisp as the folds of a starched wimple, and they never came undone. Never.

A few hours later, when I unwrapped the sandwich in the cafeteria at Ballard School, the wax paper was smooth and unwrinkled except at the ends—folded to a pattern like a paper airplane—as airtight as when it left the kitchen.

The children who brought their sandwiches with the ends of the wax paper closed in crude twists that would not hold were to be pitied. More pitiful yet were the children who brought their sandwiches in old bread wrappers. They were the children—wide cheekbones, gap-toothed, freckled, and lank-haired—who came to town on the school bus from out in the country and, thus, were called bus children. *The bus children.* There are worlds in those three words. The arms and bony legs of the bus children were inevitably daubed with gentian violet against the perpetual bloom of ground itch and ringworm and God knows what all. Their ankles were dirty. And sometimes, in winter, there was a faint kerosene odor to them. The girls carried their nickel for milk tied up in the corner of a handkerchief, like old country women. My, my. Six years old, seven, and already a cultural anthropologist.

Well. How you wrap your sandwich counts.

Not long ago, a friend asked me when, in all the world and in all my life, I felt safest.

I knew immediately.

I saw myself waiting for my father to come home in the afternoon, watching his car pull into the driveway—a dark Chevy, I think, with running boards and a gas rationing sticker on the windshield. I would run out to meet him, and we would come into the house together. Then he would go his way and I would return to my world, which involved, at that time of day, listening to radio shows—*Jack Armstrong, the All-American Boy, Sky King, Smilin' Jack*—or climbing trees, or planning to steal the neighbor's boat and run away like Huck Finn, or keeping an eye out for the Japanese invasion.

That wasn't real likely, not on the Florida Gulf Coast. But we had a neighbor who mumbled darkly that if they came—when they came—he was ready for them. The vanguard of the survivalists, I guess. My father said he was nuts, to stay away from his house, there was practically nothing on earth less likely to happen than a Japanese invasion steaming up the Manatee River.

That's not to say that we were not prepared for other enemies.

Our town had air raids and air-raid wardens and civilian air-defense watchers. The watchers went up into a tower every night at The Pier—the municipal marina that was itself a memorial to Bradenton men who died in World War I, mostly of influenza, but one or two in the trenches. There was a pseudo-Spanish, Florida boom-era tile and stucco building in the center of the pier that housed a dark little museum of local Indian artifacts and World War I ordnance and that had a tower on one corner. The airplane spotters' headquarters was in the tower. There were first-aid supplies up there, including some canvas stretchers and buckets of sand, in case of fire, and shallow, dough-boy-era helmets and binoculars. Each night the tower was manned, and watchers logged the planes that flew by and identified them as ours or theirs. They were always ours.

I still have a little lapel emblem that belonged to my father, an official memento of those years. Gold wings with a white-and-blue enamel insignia between the wings acknowledge his work as an Army Air Forces Observer.

I wear it sometimes.

I can't pin it on without countless images rushing back to me, of how bright the nights were when he let me go with him to the watchtower, of how we all learned to know a P-38 when we saw it, or a P-51, or a B-25, or a B-17, or, finally, the legendary B-29s.

The War.

It pervaded our days and nights, our school work and our play, our imaginations and our family life.

There was an Army camp in Bradenton, a staging area, I believe, for troops on their way overseas. Every Sunday we collected a couple of soldiers from church and brought them home for Sunday dinner. Fried chicken. Mashed potatoes.

Green beans. Biscuits. It sounds like a *Saturday Evening Post* cover, a Frank Capra movie. Now that we are far past innocence, it's easy to dismiss that particular brand of innocence, that world according to the forties, as illusion.

Oh no. It was real. The soldiers really came home with us to fried chicken and my parents referred to them as boys and they said yes ma'am and no sir and sometimes gave me collar emblems from their uniforms, or rating stripes they must have brought along from the PX on the chance of a dinner invitation and a household child hungry for a souvenir. Once I got a cap, one of the flat, folding caps the boys tucked into their web belts with the shiny brass buckles.

God, they were glamorous, the boys of '44.

About midafternoon, it would be time to drive the boys back to the base and I always rode along, and we let them out at the gate and they waved and I waved.

I don't remember ever having the same soldiers twice.

Odd.

We must have, but I don't remember it that way. I remember a parade, a procession of new boys, a new pair every Sunday, on their way to war.

We collected scrap metal.

We saved big balls of tinfoil that we peeled off gum wrappers.

We went without bubble gum.

We bought War Bonds—filled books of stamps, at a rate of ten cents a week, until we had $18.75 and could trade in the book for a twenty-five-dollar bond.

There were incentive programs.

Once a bomb casing was brought to the front hall at Ballard School, and the children who bought stamps were allowed to write something on the bomb casing. It was our impression that this very bomb would be eventually loaded into a bomb bay of a "Flying Fortress," on an island somewhere in the Pacific, messages scrawled in childish hands intact, and dropped with pinpoint precision onto Hirohito's lap.

The artistic among us drew caricatures of evil-looking

little devils with buckteeth and slanty eyes and the combat-ready among us got straight to the point: *Death to Japs,* we printed in white chalk. The patriots drew American flags. The poets tried to find something to rhyme with blast . . . smash . . . bust . . . explode . . . bang . . . boom . . . I came up with Ballard Bomb Go Blow TOJO. Underlined. I added a V-dot-dot-dot-dash for good measure.

When I told about the soldiers bringing the bomb to school, and the people who bought stamps being allowed to write a message to the enemy on it, my father wanted to know more about that, and I could tell by his tone that he did not approve.

I was baffled, defensive.

He said it wasn't fitting, little children writing death messages on a bomb.

But the Japanese were the enemy, weren't they? We wanted to win the war, didn't we?

Children writing on bombs was inappropriate, he said, and he intended to call the school and get to the bottom of this.

I was humiliated.

Then.

Oh, but now—the details we can add to the past, the spaces and shadows and silences we can fill, the layers and layers of what was really going on that are revealed when we revisit the moments that we call up with the interior replay button.

I can revisit that very day, feel the chalk in my hand, scratching *V-dot-dot-dot-dash* against the cold, resistant, pebbly surface of the bomb casing, revisit my telling of the day's events to my father, revisit my confusion, resentment of his response. But now I'm watching and listening, and I'm in both our heads, I am the child and I am the parent.

I hope what they say about heaven is true. I'd like to see that man again someday.

Gold wings.

A cigar tin.

Wax paper.

There is an old director's chair too.

He always sat in it out under the porte-cochere when he grilled. He liked the chair so much that when it wore out, he got it reinforced and recovered and upgraded with a bit of upholstery padding.

When the children were little and we would go down to see my parents, he would often already have the fire going by the time we turned into the driveway. He would be sitting in that director's chair, wearing a white apron with *Duffy's Tavern* stitched in red, sipping some George Dickel on the rocks, watching the fire burn down to perfect.

He was seventy years old when he died, on the night of March 16, 1969.

The next morning, driving from Jacksonville to Bradenton, it did not seem real, it did not seem possible. I had the facts, the particulars, the time and cause of death in my mind. I had talked with the children, calmly, about the things children need to know the first time they encounter death.

I was so cerebral and reasonable, so busy being strong and practical that I did not understand that I had not encountered my father's death at all, not really.

I encountered his death when we turned into the driveway and the director's chair was there, empty.

I still have the chair, and we often pull it out when we cook on the grill. It's kind of a tradition.

I think of him every day.

And, every now and then, suddenly, unexpectedly, I see him in some corner of my life.

17

Walk down the middle of the main street in Hitchcock, South Dakota, and your feet crunch in the gravel.

It's a cowboy sound.

Or maybe it's only an echo from a cowboy movie. The soundtrack needs the pocket-change jingle from a pair of spurs, the soft snort of a horse hitched to the hitching post.

There aren't any hitching posts in Hitchcock.

There aren't any parking meters either, nor any rules about where to park. If they take a notion, people can stop their pickups in the middle of the broad main street and crunch over to the Hitchcock Cafe for a beer, or into the P.O. to check the mail, or to the beauty parlor, in a weathered trailer next to the general store, for a shampoo and set.

There's a well-tended old Methodist church in Hitchcock, and a school—home of the Hitchcock Blue Jays—and a grain elevator and a couple of lighted ball fields. The tall grass that waves across the prairie like the surface of a green sea pushed by a freshening wind laps at the edge of town.

They could shoot a Chevy commercial in Hitchcock—the heartbeat of America—and kick up a fine plume of pink dust on that gravel road.

A place, like good wine, needs a certain complexity to define it, to set it apart from other places. In the South much of our character comes from the people and the ways we have devised of living together. In the Dakotas the character of the place comes from the land.

Obviously, every place has an horizon, the spot in the distance where the earth seems to end and the sky to begin. In South Dakota it looks like the horizon takes in more territory than it does in the east. For one thing, 360 degrees of the horizon is visible. There are not enough trees or towns or much of anything else to get in the way. The prairie rolls off in every direction and, way off, the sky closes down over it like the inside of a big blue mixing bowl.

In South Dakota the land is a mighty presence.

"I've ridden over a lot of this territory on a saddle horse," MelJay Hathaway said, nodding and moving a big hand in a gesture that took in a rolling sprawl of pastureland bisected by the narrow road from Wessington Springs to Gann Valley. Well-favored cattle, like those cows in the Pharaoh's dream, grazed across green land that folded gently around a series of deep, grassy gullies. Straw-colored tumbleweeds were piled up along a barbed-wire fence.

"Working stock," he added, a few miles down the road. "I've worked stock all over this country."

He didn't mean all over America. He meant all over the country that we passed through, the rolling land that surrounded us like the sea.

We were on our way to Elm Creek. "Elm Crick," they say in South Dakota. In 1883 two brothers homesteaded on Elm Crick. One of them was my grandfather, Homer Dye. He and my grandmother, Marie, didn't stay in South Dakota. In a few years they returned to Iowa.

But Homer's brother and sister-in-law, Trippett and Annie Dye, stayed. Every June, Trippett and Annie's descendants gather in a park in Wessington Springs for a cousins' picnic. They reminisce about their grandmother and their grandfather and the old days in the big house on Elm Creek. Their children and grandchildren listen to the stories and stay connected to the family, to Elm Creek, to one another.

The family has its own mythology, its own heroes, its own tall tales.

All families do.

But the tales and recollections of these western cousins intrigue me because they are so entwined with the American myths that we all share, wherever, however, whenever we grew up.

Cowboys. Indians. Homesteaders. Wagon trains. The plow that broke the plains. Drought and blizzard. Cattle drives. The indomitable pioneer women. Range wars. Wolves, buffaloes, rattlesnakes. Gunslingers and outlaws and lawmen. The coming of the railroad.

Sitting in the dark at Saturday matinees from Key West to Brooklyn, we learned it all from the movies. And even before the movies, there were pulp novels and, for that matter, good novels—*The Virginian, Little House on the Prairie*—of how the West was won.

We recognize the West when we see it, even when we see it for the first time, because it's already there in the imagination, right down to the way footsteps crunch on gravel.

It is the sound of the lone sheriff stepping out to confront chaos.

High Noon.

Soundtracks.

The pattern again, the image.

Would I have fallen in love with Henry Hyman on that December afternoon on the train platform in Jacksonville, Florida, if I had never seen *Casablanca?* Do Joseph and Elizabeth Hyman, and Jessica Hyman, exist because, once upon a time, Henry and I happened through the edge of a movie plot and remembered what was supposed to happen, remembered our lines? *Here's looking at you, kid.*

What an odd thought! Is it possible? And would it make life more patterned or more random than we believe it to be? What would it say of the essence of our relationships?

I don't know.

But there it is.

Sometime during the 1920s, the Lady Helpers of the First Congregational Church of Gann Valley asked the pioneers of Buffalo County to recollect the early days.

Here is what the Dyes wrote:

> *Forty years ago, the country was one great stretch of prairie as far as you could see with, once in a while, a claim shanty. A little before sundown, we reached a high hill which gave us a splendid view of Elm Creek. Trippett stopped the team, put his arm around me and said, Does it look good to you, little girl? After riding all day over 40 miles of prairie, it looked beautiful. It looks good to me yet.*
>
> *We picked out our location and started our home. It was 12 feet square and the roof slanted north and south, one window in the east and a door on the south. The sides were 8-inch ship lap and were nailed up and down. The wind found its way through the cracks right soon.*

They wrote:

> *Hot winds almost like the blasts from a red hot furnace continued day after day. Vegetation burned and withered and there was practically neither hay nor crops of any kind and these conditions brought about much hardship and suffering. This portion of the country was almost depopulated and deserted homestead shacks on every hand told a bitter tale of shattered hopes. Elm Creek valley, which at one time was the liveliest and loveliest spot on the map, was lonely and forsaken.*

We turned off the highway onto a gravel road that led down to the place on Elm Creek where Homer and Trippett had had their homesteads, Trippett on the east bank, Homer on the west. No one knows anymore exactly where Homer and Marie built their claim shack.

"I've always thought it must have been right about there"—Hathaway pointed to a level spot close to the creek.

"And the baby, Little Soldier, he's buried over there somewhere. They buried him on the prairie," added Grace Dye Hathaway. She is Trippett and Annie's granddaughter, one of the organizers of the cousins' picnic.

Little Soldier.

His name was Waldo Homer Dye, and he lived only four months, through the summer of 1885, from June until October.

Annie, the baby's aunt, wrote:

> *Homer and Marie had awakened and found him dead. They had done all they could for him, but it was heart failure. The next afternoon, they had the funeral in the house. They picked out a pretty spot about three-quarters of a mile away from here, a sad and sympathetic crowd saw Little Soldier lowered into his last resting place. There were no graveyards here at that time . . .*

Every year, at the cousins' picnic, someone remembers Waldo and wonders where he is buried, and every year Grace Hathaway cries when she thinks about him. People kind of tease her about that, but she doesn't mind. She cries anyway.

Marie, my grandmother, died in 1905 and until that day in South Dakota she had been no more to me than a face in an old photograph that hung in my parents' bedroom, in the corner, over the sewing machine. Waldo had been no more than a name, and I had never known his nickname: Little Soldier.

I knew the fact, that he died in infancy in South Dakota. But I did not know his story.

I did not know the story until I stood at Elm Creek and

looked west, across the prairie. I thought of Homer and Marie and of Waldo, of the tiny bones on the endless prairie.

There were no graveyards here at that time . . .

I thought of burying a baby where there were no graveyards.

They picked out a pretty spot . . .

We need to know the stories, all the stories, and to tell them to one another around whatever passes for a campfire these days.

We've come a long way together, and we ought not to forget.

They wrote: *The memory of the struggles and the action clings resolutely and tenderly in the minds of the men and women who have been through things and won.*

Yes.

We have been through things and won.

I crossed Elm Creek and stopped the car and walked back to the little wooden bridge that spanned it. Birds, some sort of big black birds, exploded up from the grass at the edge of the creek and climbed into the red sky that closed down over the plains like a distant curtain across a stage. The birds hung against the sky for a moment, skimmed into the sun and were gone. I wanted to climb down off the bridge and walk along the bank of the creek and find a pretty spot and sit quietly for a while and just be with them, with Homer and Marie and Waldo.

I thought that, if I found the right spot and if I were quiet, they would come, and, one by one, the others, too, until there would be a great multitude of us there by Elm Creek, and that somebody would pick up a fiddle . . .

They wrote:

> *They came on foot, on horseback, with ox teams, wagons, carts, and, occasionally, a vehicle dignified by the name of a buggy. All brought their dinners, came early and stayed late. The Fourth of July oration was considered an important part of the pro-*

gram. The celebration always closed with a
big dance with music by the fiddle.

But there was no time to wait.

The light was almost gone, retreating across the prairie.

I took a couple of snapshots of Elm Creek and then I followed the road back the way I had come, traveling toward home.

ABOUT THE AUTHOR

Ann Hyman writes for the *Florida Times-Union* and has traveled extensively, including a stay in the Soviet Union as part of a journalistic exchange. She lives in Jacksonville, Florida.